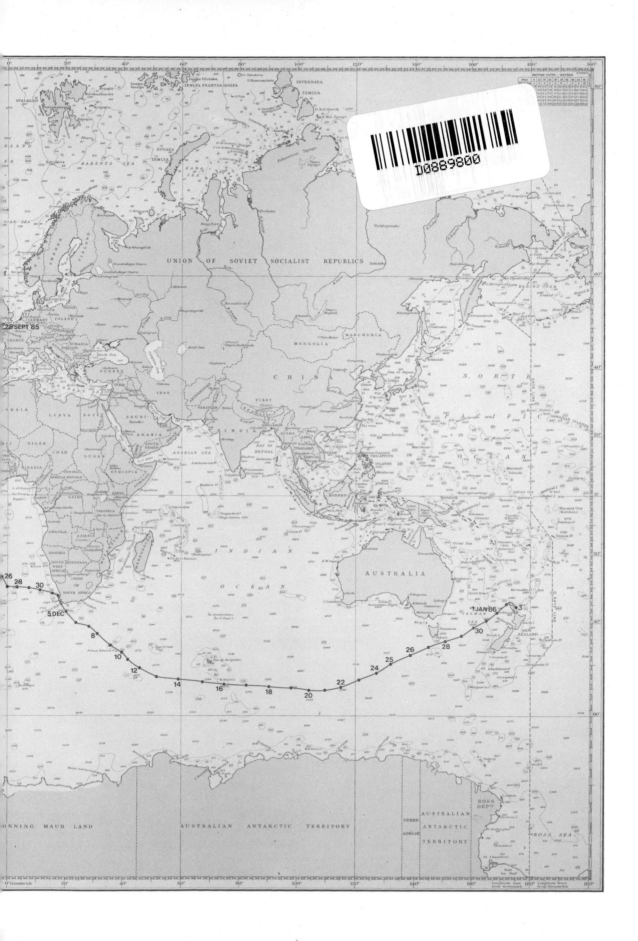

LION

Other books by Peter Blake

Blake's Odyssey (with Alan Sefton)
Peter Blake's Yachting Book (with David Pardon)

LION
THE ROUND THE WORLD RACE
WITH LION NEW ZEALAND

PETER BLAKE • ALAN SEFTON

HODDER AND STOUGHTON
AUCKLAND LONDON SYDNEY TORONTO

To Pippa and Sarah-Jane
To Nora, Kel, Leon and Justine

Copyright © 1986 Peter Blake and Alan Sefton
First published 1986
ISBN 0 340 401141

Book design, maps and typesetting by Acorn Graphics Ltd, Auckland.
Printed and bound in Hong Kong for Hodder and Stoughton Ltd, View Road, Glenfield, Auckland, New Zealand.

Contents

Appendices: • 1985-86 Whitbread Race Awards
 • Previous Whitbread Race Winners
 • N.Z. International Yacht Racing
 Trust Committee and Trustees
 • Main Sponsors of *Lion New Zealand*
 • Trade Suppliers and Project Supporters
 • Captain's Club Members
 • Admiral's Club Members
 • Former *Ceramco* shareholders who transferred their
 interest to *Lion*

Acknowledgements

This book is the story of a boat and a project which cost several million dollars and was 2½ years in the making and doing.

No such undertaking would be possible without the unstinting support of a great many people. Sir Thomas Clark made it all happen with his special mix of commercial clout, energy and charisma. His back-up team included Alan Topham, OBE, John Balgarnie, Mike Clark, Jock O'Connor, Mark van Praagh and Sylvia Dunbar, who all contributed above and beyond the call of duty. There was the personal and material support of good friends, Alan Gibbs and Ken Lusty.

The major sponsors, headed by Douglas Myers and New Zealand Breweries Ltd and Lion Corporation, broke new ground in this venture. They were Air New Zealand (Norman Geary, Richard Gates, Bob Wallace and Garry Court), Atlas Corporation (Charles Bidwell), Auckland Coin & Bullion Exchange (Ray Smith), Chase Corporation (Colin Reynolds), Construction Machinery Ltd (Geoff Clark), Fay, Richwhite (Michael Fay and David Richwhite), Healing Industries Ltd (Trevor Geldard and Ron Brown), John Andrew Ford (Neville Crichton and Colin Giltrap), McConnell Dowell Corporation (Malcolm McConnell and Jim Dowell), Mogal Corporation (Bob Owens, Bob Sylvester and Clive Bennett), New Zealand Line (Charles Speight and Chris Cooney), and The Newmans Group (Peter Grayburn).

To all of them, and to the subsidiary sponsors and contributors listed in the appendices to the *Lion* story, we would like to say a personal thank you. We set out to achieve excellence in everything related to the boat and her campaign. With their help we succeeded, generating a wealth of international plaudits for New Zealand in the process.

In the production of this book, we had invaluable assistance from a number of people but especially Tom Beran, of Hodder and Stoughton, who toiled long and hard to keep us on schedule. Pam Prior transcribed the taped log from which the racing chapters were reconstructed, and Maggie Kerrigan, of Air New Zealand, took a special interest in the whole project from the outset.

Lastly, thanks to the people of New Zealand who take such an interest in events such as the Whitbread race. Their financial contributions were greatly appreciated but probably more so were the reception and the farewell that they gave the fleet in Auckland. Nobody who sailed in the race will ever forget those heady occasions, or the generosity and hospitality of a nation whose awareness of yacht racing is unique.

The publisher gratefully acknowledges the assistance of Air New Zealand in the production of this book.

The photographs in this book are the work of Alan Sefton, Rob Tucker, Godfrey Cray, Daniel Forster, Bruce Woods, Bret de Thier, Fraser Maxwell, Paul von Zalinsky, Ian Mainsbridge and Judy Glanville.

Unfinished Business

Tuesday, 30 March 1982: *Ceramco New Zealand* hardened up into the squally south-westerly and powered towards the Whitbread Round the World race finish-line off the entrance to Portsmouth Harbour. It was shortly before one o'clock in the morning and bitterly cold. But nobody paid any heed to the time or the elements. The 'Porcelain Rocketship' — a nickname for the 68ft Farr design which alluded to both her main sponsor and to her performance — had a bone in her teeth and was poised to again prove what might have been.

Ceramco was not the first yacht to complete the epic 27,000-mile journey. That honour had gone to the 76ft Frers design *Flyer* 17 hours earlier. Immaculately prepared and campaigned by Dutchman Conny van Rietschoten, *Flyer* had been first across the line in all four legs of this ocean-racing classic. But she had been given a race to end all races by the smaller New Zealand yacht and what counted now for Peter Blake and his crew was that *Ceramco* had beaten *Flyer* for the third leg in a row on corrected time. This is the handicap system which enables big and small boats to race equitably against one another despite the differences in their dimensions.

A bigger boat should always beat a smaller one, the theoretical speed of a hull being a function of its waterline length. To accommodate this, the rulemakers of the sport have evolved a complicated formula which assesses the speed-producing and drag-inducing features of a yacht and expresses its evaluation in a foot rating. This foot rating is in turn converted into a time-correction factor which is applied to a yacht's elapsed time in a race, or in a leg of a race, like the Whitbread. The outcome is a yacht's corrected time and the winner of a race, or a leg, is the yacht with the lowest corrected result.

The glamour maxi yachts, first into port, claim much of the publicity that attends major ocean-racing events like the Whitbread, but the corrected time victory is the real prize. Since leaving Cape Town some 20,000 miles and five months earlier, *Ceramco* had won two of the three legs on corrected time and had built up a handicap margin of 29 hours 23 minutes on *Flyer*.

But, in the final analysis of the race, these were to prove battle statistics only. *Flyer* won the war. She was not only fastest around the world with an elapsed time of 120 days 6 hours 34 minutes (a full 14 days 5 hours quicker than the previous record), but she also had the best corrected time to complete the coveted line and handicap double.

Although *Ceramco* had performed brilliantly from Cape Town to the finish, she was unable to overcome the loss of her rig just 23 days into the race when she was pacing *Flyer* down the South Atlantic in the first leg from Portsmouth to Cape Town. In real terms, *Ceramco's* race had finished then and there, 120 miles north of Ascension Island. Blake's years of planning and fundraising, of commitment and endeavour, had been betrayed by a failure of her stainless steel rod rigging. Without the necessary support, the mast crumpled and bent in two places. Cape Town was still 2500 miles away and *Ceramco* was a lame duck.

Most people would have quit if faced with such daunting circumstances. But Blake and his crew fashioned an ingenious makeshift mast from the tangled remains of the original spar and doggedly refused to concede. They couldn't sail efficiently to windward, and it was to windward that Cape Town lay by the shortest route. So Blake laid a course that was favoured by the famous clipper ships of old, around the 'back' of the notorious South Atlantic High in search of a greater predominance of tailwinds. The route was anything from 1000 to 1500 miles longer, but with luck *Ceramco* would still make reasonable time even with her greatly reduced and inefficient sail plan.

Twenty-four days and 4000 miles later, *Ceramco* limped into Cape Town. Incredibly, she managed to beat eight of the 26 starters to the Cape of Good Hope. But despite a marvellous effort by Blake and his team, *Ceramco* was 10 days 20 hours behind *Flyer* on elapsed time and last in the fleet on corrected time.

The deficit was too great to be overcome. That didn't mean it couldn't be attacked though. *Ceramco* chased *Flyer* through the Southern Ocean in a unique match race that shattered records and kept the population of New Zealand on the edge of its seat. After 7010 miles from Cape Town to Auckland, the two boats were only 8 hours and 20 minutes apart arriving in *Ceramco's* home port. The local boat was given a tremendous reception by Auckland's boating-mad public who turned out in their thousands to let Blake's team know that what they were doing was appreciated.

Ceramco New Zealand . . . left unfinished business.

The mad-dash match race continued from Auckland to Mar del Plata, in Argentina, as *Flyer* and *Ceramco* averaged 10 knots for the 6000-mile journey. They had each other in sight for 10 days and 2500 miles on the way to Cape Horn, rounded that historic landmark just three miles apart and reached Mar del Plata within 7 hours 17 minutes of each other.

Back up through the Atlantic, the chase was on again. The margin between the two boats at the Portsmouth finish was 17 hours 9 minutes, after 6600 miles — the furthest the two yachts had been apart since leaving Cape Town.

Ceramco had achieved much. She'd conceded *Flyer* eight feet in length yet paced her mile for mile through the world's most desolate and demanding oceans. She'd won two legs on corrected time and picked up the Roaring Forties Trophy for being the top boat through the Southern Ocean in legs two and three. And she'd finished third fastest around the world, breaking the previous record in the process, despite sailing 4000 miles under jury rig on the way to Cape Town.

Blake had a lot to reflect on as the welcome party in Portsmouth raged on through the night. This had been his third Whitbread and, he told interviewers, his last. This was as good a time as any to call it quits. He had given the world's greatest yacht race, one of the last of the great adventures some called it, his best shot. But had he?

As he chatted with his major sponsor, managing director of the Ceramco group of companies, Tom Clark, the party going on all around, the conversation centred on what might have been had *Ceramco*'s rig not folded in leg one. Although neither of them would admit it for some months to come, Blake and Clark had been discussing what they would later term 'unfinished business'.

In that crowded, noisy bar in a distant land, in the wee small hours of the morning, another major Kiwi challenge for the Round the World race was conceived. The progeny would be a Lion . . .

Ron Holland

1. Design Dilemma

I don't think Tom Clark or I made a conscious decision to put a campaign together for the 1985-86 Whitbread race. It was something that evolved as we tidied up the loose ends of the 1981-82 effort.

We were luckier than most other competitors in that we found fairly quickly a buyer for *Ceramco*. She was a steal at US$480,000 and Californian Hal Day got a real bargain, a downwind thoroughbred which had been beautifully built and faithfully maintained. Day had the Transpac (Los Angeles to Honolulu) race and the Clipper Cup series in Hawaii in mind and *Ceramco*, renamed *Winterhawk*, offered some exciting prospects with the downwind speed she'd shown in the Round the World duel with *Flyer*.

The sale was cleverly organised, however, and while Day picked up a bargain, the *Ceramco* trust back in New Zealand got the money it needed to emerge from the campaign with a final balance sheet entry that was in black ink. One of the details that then had to be attended to was the reimbursement of the 420-odd debenture holders in the boat. Tom found that the majority of these 'syndicate' members would be quite amenable to rolling their $500 into a new campaign fund. It doesn't take Tom long to start things moving in such circumstances.

In the meantime, I was fully recovered from what I can only describe as post-Whitbread depression. When you've lived through a project as intense as the *Ceramco* campaign for more than two years, and when you've raced a boat 24 hours a day, seven days a week for the best part of seven months around the world, it takes time to come down to earth again and for your ocean-racing appetite to return. Warm, dry beds that don't move are a luxury that quickly grow on you. So is a varied diet of fresh food. And so is the opportunity to walk around the corner to your local if you feel like a beer, or to dine with friends at your favourite restaurant.

But when you have lived on an adrenalin high such as the real buzz that racing *Ceramco* through the Southern Ocean provided, you forget the discomforts and the misery of a Whitbread race. Your memory conveniently erases the bad times and calls up only the good. It's not the Chinese gybe which had *Ceramco* lying on her ear and in real danger, thousands of miles from the closest land, that you remember. It's the 300-mile days, the roller-coaster rides through big seas in gale- and even storm-force tailwinds, the excitement of arriving in Auckland, the anticipation of visiting exotic-sounding ports.

My 'cure' was hastened by the writing of *Blake's Odyssey*, the book which told the story of *Ceramco New Zealand* and her somewhat dramatic 1981-82 Round the World race. Going through my logs, as we recounted that story, brought all the memories flooding back and by the time Tom and I next sat down for a serious discussion about the future, I found myself more than ready to do it all again. Tom had been busy. Once he determined that New Zealand and its people would support another Whitbread challenge, he set to work in earnest.

It wasn't going to be as easy next time around. When we set out on the *Ceramco* project, with Warwick White, my old friend Martin Foster, and Peter Cornes accepting the onerous task of raising the money, the thought of having to come up with $600,000 scared the living daylights out of us. Tom and the Ceramco group of companies provided much-needed relief with a major sponsorship and the good old Kiwi public did the rest as the project gained momentum and captured everyone's imagination.

For 1985-86, however, the budget would need to be a daunting $3 million. The reason for this was the worldwide reaction to the 1981-82 match race between *Flyer* and *Ceramco*, and *Flyer*'s double win. We'd proved, during that thrilling encounter, that well-campaigned bigger boats were capable of pacing the weather systems through the Southern Ocean, staying with those systems and doing tremendous daily runs for weeks at a time. Smaller yachts, without the same speed potential, could not keep up with the systems and inevitably got left a long way behind with no chance of saving their time on handicap.

This being the case, the only way to go in 1985-86 was full-on at the top end of the size range. That meant a maxi of around 80ft overall length — and all that went with it. The cost of such an undertaking does not increase proportionately. It triples and quadruples. You can't walk in and buy everything off the shelf for an 80-footer. Much of the gear has to be custom-made, especially when you are going to race that 80-footer around the world. So your equipment costs considerably more.

The same is true in every other area. Maxis need more crew, and more crew

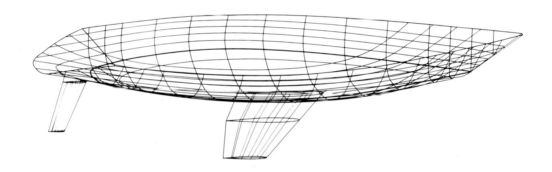

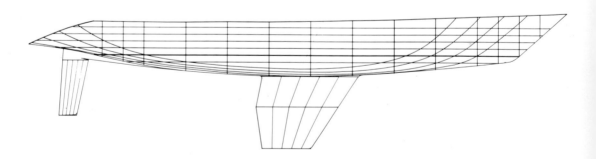

*Computer projections of **Lion New Zealand**'s lines illustrate an easily driven, slim-bodied hull with few rating distortions to detract from good handling characteristics.*

means more food, water, medical supplies, clothing, air fares, shore accommodation and so on. A 20ft container to ship your spares to the ports of call becomes a 40ft container and because maxis are hard on gear, your spares list needs to be extensive. You can't buy the gear you need in most ports of call, so you have to send it on ahead of you to ensure that you don't get caught short for any particular item. You need different sails for different legs, particularly mainsails. A mainsail in Kevlar for a maxi costs in excess of $30,000, but you have to replace as you go even if the costs are high. Sails are your motive force and you can't cut corners.

Fully aware of the ramifications of a decision to go big, Tom Clark knew that funding would be critical and would have to be approached differently to the *Ceramco* exercise. His solution was to solicit corporate sponsorship to cover the costs of building and equipping a maxi. No decision to go again in 1985-86 would be contemplated until these sponsorships were secured.

His targets defined, Tom went quietly but resolutely about his business. There was no publicity, no drum-beating. This was an exercise which had to be accomplished in secret. If Tom was successful in securing the best part of $1.5 million, the challenge would be announced. If he wasn't, nobody would know any different and the project would be shelved. Selecting his 'marks' with great care and handling the approaches personally, Tom slowly but surely assembled the support we required. There can be few more charismatic people in New Zealand commerce or sport than Tom Clark. A self-made man, he has been a success at virtually everything he has tackled, be that big business, international motor racing or international yacht racing. When he fronts up and argues that something needs to be done and can be done, backing what he says with his own formidable track record, people tend to sit up and take notice.

The upshot was that in remarkably short time, even by his standards, Tom had assembled a sponsorship package which satisfied him. Most of the money to build and equip a maxi was either to hand or in view. Lion Breweries, the country's biggest beer producer and now under the leadership of Douglas Myers, one of the so-called young turks who were reshaping the business image of New Zealand, bought naming rights and became the biggest single backer of the project. In one stroke of entrepreneurial genius, Tom had secured not only a major portion of the money required to build a boat but also a nationwide chain of outlets through which public fundraising for campaign costs could be carried out. In behind the brewery were 12 of New Zealand's more progressive companies and corporations, signed on as subsidiary sponsors — Air New Zealand, the Atlas Corporation, Auckland Coin and

Tom Clark

Douglas Myers

13

Bullion Exchange, the Chase Corporation, Construction Machinery Ltd, Fay, Richwhite & Co., the Mogal Corporation, Healing Industries, McConnell Dowell Corporation, John Andrew Ford, the Shipping Corporation of New Zealand, and Newmans.

It was an interesting mix ranging from New Zealand's national air and shipping lines, a privately owned and hugely influential merchant bank, a newly listed property development and investment company, an international construction group, an internationally renowned marine paint manufacturer and the country's biggest motor trade dealership. By the time Tom contacted me with the green light to pursue design options, Air New Zealand, Atlas Corporation, Chase, Fay, Richwhite, Healing Industries and John Andrew Ford had already signed up, as had more than 120 syndicate shareholders from the *Ceramco* project. The New Zealand International Yacht Racing Trust was being formed to fund and campaign a 1985-86 Whitbread challenger with a projected budget of $2.25 million.

While I was charged with deciding which maxi to build, Tom continued his quest for the wherewithal. Neither task was simple. Tom had to fully convince more business leaders of the merit of committing not inconsiderable sums of money to an intangible project, the outcome of which would always be uncertain given the nature of ocean racing generally and the Whitbread race in particular.

I, meanwhile, had to canvas the world's leading yacht designers to ensure that the boat we built would live up to the expectations of those investing in it. As with *Ceramco*, there were original basic criteria. We wanted this to be another all-Kiwi project involving a boat designed by New Zealanders, built in New Zealand and raced by New Zealanders. If we were to excite public interest at home, the project would need to involve a strong nationalistic theme. The obvious contenders for the design commission were Bruce Farr and Ron Holland, both leaders in the field while working outside of their native New Zealand — Farr based in Annapolis on the eastern seaboard of the United States, Holland tucked away in Currabinny, on the banks of Cork Harbour in southern Ireland. But while we wanted to be patriotic in our design decision, we also had to be thorough and practical. An all-Kiwi approach was a good selling-point, but we would look mugs if we turned our backs on something better from a design office which didn't have New Zealand connections.

To occupy my mind while waiting for *Ceramco* to sell, I'd begun putting together the beginnings of another Whitbread project. Tom was not involved at that stage and my tentative feelers for potential sponsors were not restricted to New Zealand. During this very low-key process, I got in touch with most of the world's top design offices to tell them what might develop and what I had in mind. There were no commitments or commissions in view at that stage. I was simply testing the water, so to speak.

The designers I had most dealings with were German Frers, Ed Dubois, Bruce Farr and Ron Holland. Frers, an Argentinian who did his training in the famous Sparkman and Stephens office in New York, was emerging as the world's leading big-boat designer. After *Flyer*'s success in the 1981-82 Whitbread, he followed up with circuit maxis — the big boats that concentrate on the shorter classics in world ocean racing, races like the Fastnet and the Sydney-Hobart — which had real potential. Dubois was a young Englishman who had broken into the design spotlight with *Victory*, the outstanding boat in the 1981 Admiral's Cup, and then produced the very promising *Indulgence* for the 1983 season in Britain. He had some interesting ideas for a Whitbread maxi and I spent a lot of time exploring these with him.

Then there were the Kiwis, Farr and Holland. These two came from different

Kialoa displayed some disastrous downwind characteristics in Hawaii.

ends of the design spectrum. Farr had made his name with light, downwind machines while Holland was more into displacement. Farr obviously had to be high on the list. *Ceramco* had turned out to be everything that we'd asked for, even though I now had some different ideas on what was required to win a round-the-world race.

At that stage, I wasn't really keen to consider Holland. He had been the first designer to improve the maxi scene with his 79ft *Kialoa* for Jim Kilroy, the Californian property developer who was the dominating influence in maxi affairs. He followed *Kialoa* with *Condor,* for England's Bob Bell. Those two boats were streets ahead of anything else, at the time, particularly going to windward. But they had performed in alarming fashion in Hawaii in the 1982 Clipper Cup series. In strong winds from behind they were totally out of control and you couldn't even contemplate a yacht with that sort of handling problem for the Southern Ocean, which dictates that you have a boat which is very controllable and runs and surfs well. There were other designers on my list, but most of them were ruled out by the fact that they either hadn't done the Whitbread before or they had no experience or track record with maxis.

When *Ceramco* sold and we got down to the nitty-gritty with a New Zealand project headed by Tom Clark, the decision as to which design office to use was narrowed down to a choice between Farr and Holland. I still wasn't all that keen on a Holland boat but had been having talks with him about a possible 80ft multihull in which one could attempt a non-stop round-the-world record. I referred to it as my 'Round the World in 80 Days' project. In the process of those talks I saw what Holland was doing with a 1985-86 Whitbread boat, which was to be called *Colt Cars*, and with some light displacement, downwind flyers for the United States. His concepts seemed to be very good so the lines of communication were kept open.

At the same time, we were continuing discussions with the Farr office in Annapolis. I had, by now, done a lot more work on what I wanted for a Whitbread maxi and detailed my thinking to Farr and his design team. *Ceramco* was an extremely good vessel but there were certain points that we wanted corrected. Farr was really keen to do the boat and we made solid progress in our negotiations until we struck the question of exclusivity. Both Tom and myself wanted a one-off, a maxi which was the product of our input and experience allied to the design abilities of the Farr team. We wanted the only such maxi in the Whitbread race.

The Farr office, however, was already committed to designing Whitbread maxis for two other customers and all they were prepared to offer was the same hull with small modifications towards our design criteria. We had a problem. We didn't want anyone else getting the advantage of our thinking. We asked what it would cost to buy exclusivity. The answer was a figure which was prohibitive. Tom and I saw red. We could understand the Farr point of view to a degree. But the *Ceramco* project had done a lot of good for the Farr office and we felt they might have been somewhat more generous towards us.

Faced with this situation, we decided to approach the Holland office with a strict set of design criteria to see if they could produce what we had in mind. Those criteria were for a boat of between 30 and 31 tons actual displacement which was light but very stiff. It would have to excel to windward and be very fast when two-sail reaching. But it would also have to be quick and fully controllable downwind with a spinnaker on.

Holland had already designed *Colt Cars*, a 77-footer, for Rob James, husband of New Zealand's Dame Naomi, who skippered *GB II* in a then record circumnavigation

LION NEW ZEALAND

Length overall:	23.93m	78ft 6in
Waterline length:	19.96m	65ft 6in
Beam:	5.64m	18ft 6in
Draft:	3.96m	13ft
Displacement:	32.205 tonnes	31.7 tons
Ballast:	13.71 tonnes	13.5 tons
Mast height above deck:	30.48m	100ft
Sail area:		
Main sail:	138 sq m	1,485 sq ft
No. 1 genoa:	208 sq m	2,240 sq ft
No. 1 spinnaker:	452 sq m	4,864 sq ft

I.O.R. rating 67.4 ft

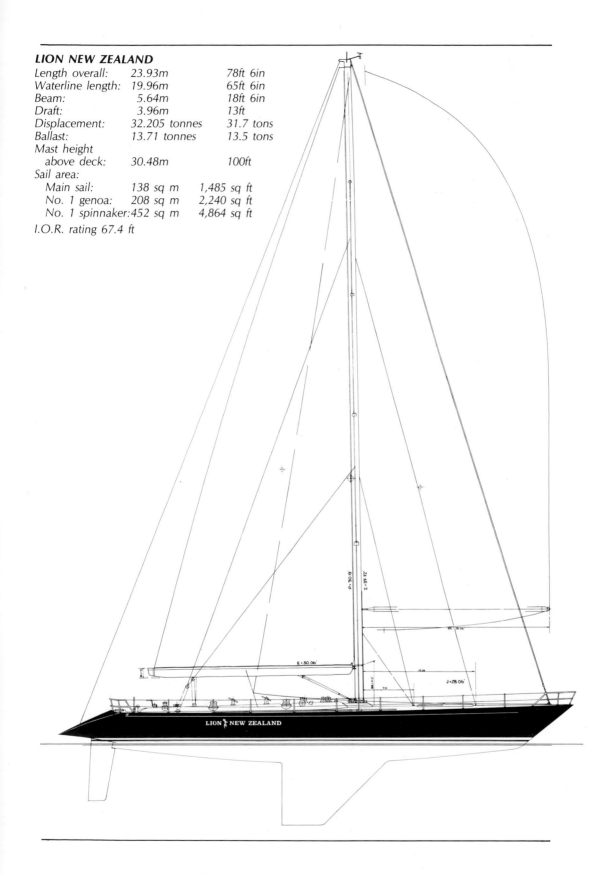

in the 1977-78 Round the World race. Rob had specified a boat not too dissimilar to the one we were seeking. Tragically, Rob drowned when he went over the side from his trimaran *Colt Cars GB* off Falmouth Harbour in March 1983. The *Colt Cars* project almost lapsed when the sponsor withdrew after Rob's death. But the boat was resurrected as *Drum England* and was to play a drama-packed role in the later scheme of things.

Our design brief to Holland involved some vital differences from the approach which almost proved to be right with *Ceramco* in 1981-82. This time I wanted a masthead rig as opposed to *Ceramco's* fractional. I was concerned about having to gybe a maxi fractional rig, with less permanent support than a masthead, in rugged conditions in the Southern Ocean and I wasn't too enamoured of the prospect of dragging a fractional rig's longer main boom through those same oceans either.

I also planned to race with a large crew to keep driving the boat at optimum speed 24 hours a day for weeks on end. The combination of a lightish boat and a large crew would not have been possible in previous races. The weight of food and water for larger numbers of people would have been prohibitive. With the advances in on-board water-makers — which convert salt water to fresh — and freeze-dried foods, that combination was now entirely feasible.

What we were really seeking was a boat with abilities and characteristics not too far removed from those of *Ceramco*. With the benefit of experience and hindsight, however, we wanted performance gains in some areas and better handling qualities in others. If we couldn't get exclusivity on that approach from Farr, we'd seek it from Holland, provided he was confident that he could design and engineer the boat we wanted in the first place.

There were those who thought we were making too big an issue of exclusivity. I didn't think so, nor did Tom. The input and information we had to offer a designer was significant and hard earned, in terms of both effort and expense. We didn't want that input available to anyone else who could come up with a design fee and commission the same design office as us.

Some people also thought we contradicted ourselves by commissioning Holland who had already done a boat for Rob James which wasn't that far from our thinking. The difference was that the Farr office would not even give us an assurance that they would work on no other Whitbread boat once they'd received our submissions and ideas and produced a design for us. This was the least we would accept if we were to feel sure that nobody else would benefit from what we had to offer. The Holland office gave us that assurance readily, together with the promise that they would have no further part in *Colt Cars* either, if or when a new owner or backers were found to rescue the mothballed hull.

Tom and I had the assurances we'd sought. The Holland office was confident it could do the boat and agreed to the exclusivity we required. We were later to discover that we in fact achieved neither of our goals. The Holland office had a major involvement in *Colt Cars* becoming *Drum England*, and even in helping to search out new owners in pop star Simon Le Bon and his business partners Paul and Mike Berrow.

And, as for the ultimate Whitbread yacht we were seeking, we finished up with a maxi which wasn't a maxi and one which instead of weighing 31 tons came in closer to 38 tons. That extra weight was in the worst possible place — in the hull and fittings, where nothing could be done about it.

Gurr

He that only rules by terror
Doeth grevious wrong
Alfred, Lord Tennyson
The Captain

2. The Lion Is Born

The design decision made, there was now much to do — organising a yard in Auckland to build the boat, selecting and ordering equipment and laying the groundwork for choosing a crew.

There were a number of top yards in New Zealand's City of Sails highly capable of building any size of yacht, among them McMullen & Wing on the Tamaki River who did such an impressive job with the aluminium-hulled *Ceramco New Zealand*. There weren't at the time, however, many which could handle the construction of a maxi in exotic fibreglass materials. With their experience of the strength-to-weight advantages of these materials, with *Kialoa* and *Condor*, the Holland office had gone for the fibreglass option.

The building system specified by the designers was tried and proven, and this was in keeping with my approach which was to eliminate the element of risk. If previous Whitbreads were anything to go by, the demands on boat and crew were going to be considerable and I could see no reason to take chances in construction by trying

19

to reinvent the wheel. In layman's terms, the building system to be used involved a composite fibreglass and core hull to keep the water out and an aluminium internal framing system to take all of the loads imposed by rig, keel and machinery.

The lay-up for the hull would involve outer and inner skins — a Kevlar cloth sandwiching a core of end-grain balsa. Kevlar is a space-age material developed originally for the manufacture of lightweight bullet-proof vests. Enormously strong yet weighing little, it was winning increasing favour in areas such as the aerospace industry, where great strength was needed but not weight. There were a variety of core materials available but the Holland office preferred balsa's lightness and resin-absorbing qualities to produce the required bonding with the Kevlar cloth.

The use of these materials involves different construction techniques to the traditional methods. Firstly a timber plug is built to the exact shape of the boat. The inside skins of the woven Kevlar cloth are stretched over the plug and impregnated with controlled amounts of resin. Left to dry, the resulting skin is literally bullet-proof.

Then comes the end-grain balsa, shaped accurately to the lines of the boat. A vacuum-pressuring system is used to ensure attachment without an excess of resin which would be extra weight. The final step is to apply the outside skins of Kevlar cloth, again using the vacuum-pressure process to achieve the necessary adhesion and resin content. By changing the amounts of the individual materials used in this process, you can achieve laminates with varying strength-to-weight properties, but basically the result should be 50 percent lighter than an aluminium equivalent with 50 percent greater impact-strength.

When the final laminate is cured, it remains only to remove the timber plug from inside the completed hull shell, before filling and finishing to achieve the desired result. The same construction method is used for the deck which is bonded to the hull after the aluminium space-frame has been fitted inside.

Seeking total control over the construction process, Tom Clark elected to set up our own yard and staff it with various specialists who would be needed to complete the entire job. We were fortunate that well-known Auckland boatbuilder Tim Gurr was available to run the yard and oversee construction, and Tom wasted no time snapping him up. Tim had built and sailed on a number of high-profile yachts to come out of Auckland in recent years, including the big Farr designs *Cotton Blossom V* and *Zamazan* and the 1981 S.&S. Admiral's Cupper *Inca*. More importantly, from our point of view, he had been imported to England in 1981 to play a big part in the construction of the trimaran *Colt Cars GB* for Rob James. This tri was designed and engineered by the Holland office, so Gurr was already familiar with the techniques that would be used and the results that would be sought.

Events were moving quickly now and, in August 1983, it was time to announce the project and let the public in on the challenge. I flew home from England for the occasion, at the Royal New Zealand Yacht Squadron, to join Tom, chairman of the newly formed New Zealand International Yacht Racing Trust, and Lion Breweries chief Douglas Myers. The boat would be called *Lion New Zealand*, after its major backer. The plugs for the hull and deck would be completed by the end of 1983, and laminating would begin in February 1984.

Lion was scheduled to go in the water early in November 1984 in time for a thorough work-up before she crossed the Tasman for a Sydney-Hobart race debut. It was much the same schedule as that for *Ceramco* in 1980, and we hoped that *Lion* could repeat *Ceramco*'s performance in her first genuinely competitive outing. That was the 1980 Sydney-Hobart classic when she became only the fourth boat in the 36-year history of the race to do the elusive line and handicap double.

While work started on the plugs for *Lion,* in a spacious new building in Poland Road on Auckland's North Shore, I returned to Britain to collect my wife Pippa and baby daughter Sarah-Jane, and to close our house at Emsworth, on the banks of Chichester Harbour near Portsmouth, for the duration of the *Lion* project. Growing up in the balmy climes of Auckland was going to be an experience for Sarah Jane, who was born in England while we were waiting to sell *Ceramco,* but would have her first birthday in New Zealand.

I had a lengthy shopping list of gear for *Lion.* The mast would be a Hood extrusion from the United States, a product already proven with *Kialoa.* It would be built by Yachtspars in Auckland with special spreader end-fittings, designed and manufactured by Panmure yachtsman and engineer, Bob Graham. We paid special attention to this area in the light of our experience with *Ceramco.* Her rig had gone over the side during the first leg of the 1981-82 Whitbread when the port lower intermediate shroud parted where it bent over the lower spreader. The break was caused by fatigue, the stainless steel rod working and then cracking on a hard spot where it turned through the spreader — in much the same way as you would break a piece of wire by bending it back and forth. To ensure there was no action replay of this problem with *Lion*, we would terminate the cap and intermediate shrouds in universal joints at the four sets of spreaders.

The winch package would come from Lewmar, in England. We'd used Lewmars on *Ceramco* and I was still of the opinion that they were the best in the world. The all-important radio gear would be an updated version of the Sailor equipment, from Denmark, which had proved so reliable on *Ceramco.* We were going a lot further down the sponsorship track this time around and good communications would be essential if we were to give the sponsors their mileage. Part of the communications package would again be the ability to link live with Radio New Zealand stations around the country. I would have the same constant update arrangements with yachting commentator Peter Montgomery as in 1981-82, going live to air whenever possible, no matter where *Lion* was at the time.

One of the highlights of the 1981-82 race was talking to Wayne Mowat on the Tonight show, networked throughout New Zealand, as *Ceramco* rounded Cape Horn. Too many skippers ignore the need for the ability to do that sort of thing. They opt for inferior or less powerful main radios in a bid to save on weight. But they will find they must be able to keep in touch with home base from any part of the world, as bigger sponsorships become a fact of life for the new breed of Whitbread maxis.

The navigation equipment would again include a satellite navigator which, by 'talking' to a system of space orbiters, would pinpoint *Lion*'s position within yards — a great boon. This time, however, the satnav would be linked directly to the computerised Brookes and Gatehouse Hercules system and an on-board Apple computer to provide us with a whole array of information on performance and progress, including optimum courses, angles of attack and speeds to be made good on any point of sail. Then, of course, there was the all-important weather facsimile receiver which would churn out the weather maps that would be vital to correct tactical decisions.

Packing all of this gear into the navigation station on the starboard side of *Lion* was going to be a complicated exercise, but it was all essential to racing at peak

The finished hull off the plug and being turned right side up.

efficiency and to ensuring that *Lion* was always going in the right direction at best possible speed, relative to the weather patterns and to the opposition. Some boats would this time also include radar in their electronics, but I didn't yet see the need for this considering the weight and windage that a transceiver on the stern would represent. Decisions on all of this equipment had to be made early, so that orders were placed in time to guarantee delivery before the gear was needed for installation.

The same was true in the sails department. A wardrobe for a maxi is a major undertaking for any loft and the extra strength and durability which has to be built into a Whitbread wardrobe poses even greater demands. For the easily driven *Ceramco* we had chosen the Lidgard Sails loft in Auckland, mainly because their top man, Jim Lidgard, was totally conversant with fractional rigs and what they dictated in sail shapes. For *Lion*'s big masthead rig, however, we preferred the maxi experience of the international Hood loft. Fraser Beer, in Auckland, would do much of the design with input from the Hood maxi yacht division in Marblehead, near Boston in the United States.

While all of this was being put into train, I began to concentrate on crew. After careful analysis of loads and weights, I decided that *Lion* would need 22 people, including myself, to race her around the world as though she were racing around the buoys. I would need a very special mix of big-boat experience, small-boat enthusiasm and real character to achieve a crew of that size, which would last the whole campaign without self-destructing.

Ceramco was again the starting point. The New Zealand boats in the 1981-82 race — *Ceramco* and Digby Taylor's 50-footer *Outward Bound* — were the only two yachts which did the full journey with the same crews. My team on *Ceramco* were something special and my recruiting drive for *Lion* started with them. The announcement that *Lion* needed a crew brought more than 150 applications from throughout New Zealand. Every one of those applicants had to be considered, but lack of big-boat or major racing experience ruled out most.

Lion was going to be a totally different proposition to *Ceramco*. *Ceramco*'s fractional rig meant that the loads imposed on gear were, relatively, not great. In that respect, she was a forgiving yacht. But *Lion* was going to be a full-on maxi. With a masthead rig and twice the sail area of *Ceramco*, she would impose brutish demands on the people who sailed her. I was going to need crew who knew what they were doing because if they didn't, someone could get hurt, or even killed.

Finding such people was difficult. New Zealand is involved in probably more racing, per capita, than any other nation in the world. It is also true that if you stick your head down the hatch of a big boat anywhere in the world you will usually find at least a couple of Kiwis in senior positions. But there were no maxis in New Zealand waters and gathering in the Kiwis running boats overseas proved nigh impossible. Most of those people are highly regarded by big-boat owners and are paid handsomely to take on the responsibilities of running multi-million-dollar racing machines. It was asking too much to expect them to come rushing home to take unpaid positions in a *Lion* campaign that would keep them totally involved for the best part of two years.

In the end, I resorted to hand-picking the crew I wanted from the cream of the offshore racing contingent resident in New Zealand. Most of these people were among the best in the world, racing One Tonners and Admiral's Cuppers — boats of between 40ft and 50ft overall — in teams' events such as the Southern Cross Cup in Australia, the Clipper Cup in Hawaii and the Admiral's Cup in Britain. They had the skills and the racing experience. They would have eight months, once we took delivery of *Lion*, to make the transition to completely competent maxi sailors.

A Whitbread crew must also have specialists with skills to service and repair the yacht and its gear — sailmakers, riggers, engineers, boatbuilders and electricians. In my view, a doctor is also essential. Categorising *Lion*'s needs in terms of those special skills, I identified the people I wanted on the boat and quietly let them know of my interest. To begin with, I had four of the *Ceramco* crew ready to go again — Simon Gundry, Paul von Zalinski, John Newton and Richard Macalister. Newt and Richard

---

Grant Dalton (Dalts), 27, company rep.

Ross Guiniven (Roscoe), 37, car dealer.

Mike Quilter (Mike), 31, sailmaker.

later withdrew in order to pursue promising careers — Newt in real estate and Richard managing the Barlow winch operation in New Zealand.

In the sailmaking department, I recruited Mike Quilter, Kevin Shoebridge, Tony Rae and Grant Spanhake. In addition to them, Grant Dalton took care of *Flyer's* wardrobe in the 1981-82 race and Ross Guiniven used to own and operate his own sailmaking loft in Auckland as well as working for Hoods. The riggers were Ed Danby and Martin Ford, while Bob Graham, Paul MacDonald and Roy Mason took care of my engineering needs. Glen Sowry and Godfrey Cray were the electricians, and Andrew Taylor the boatbuilder. That left a doctor, and I had to go to Whakatane Hospital to recruit Fraser Maxwell. Feeding such a large crew would require a trained chef, and Cole Sheehan got that job. That gave me 19 of my 22, counting myself. The other three, signed as general hands, were Ralph Lucas, Graeme Handley and Grant Davidson.

In every case, my prime considerations were sailing ability and experience plus the temperament to become part of a large group for a lengthy period. I was fortunate indeed to get the specialist skills as well without having to consider people who didn't have those qualities. I'd also taken care of the sailing needs of a boat like *Lion* with good watch-leader potential, plenty of sail trimmers, good mast men and bow men, and a lot of muscle for the grinders. Like everyone else who applied to join the crew, all of these specialist people had to fill in the application form and go through an interview. I wanted certain people, but I also had to be sure that those people were keen to be involved and would give the project total commitment. Dedication and keenness are essential to a project such as a Whitbread challenge.

With *Ceramco*, I went through a similar process and whittled a long list of potentials down to a final squad of 18 people. Only 11 of that squad would make the final crew and to arrive at that choice, I took all 18 on a tramp around Lake Waikaremoana in rugged Urewera National Park to the east of the centre of New Zealand's North Island. In the three days it took to walk around the lake, with everyone jammed into fairly primitive huts at night, I learnt a lot about people's idiosyncrasies and their ability to be a part of a group.

I considered doing the same with a squad of 40 to help determine who would sail on *Lion*. But I was conscious that this system had been tough on those who did

Fraser Maxwell (Doc), 25, house surgeon.

Simon Gundry (Si), 33, concrete contractor.

Grant Spanhake (Fuzz), 25, sailmaker.

not make the cut for *Ceramco* and many of the people who were close to being selected for *Lion* were already committed to sailing in major events, such as the Clipper Cup in Hawaii. I felt that, in most cases, sea miles were more valuable than being hauled around a remote lake. I had made the conditions for selection as tough as possible to begin with, the idea being that I could ease back a little later on knowing that I'd already signed the best and the keenest — people who would be under no illusions as to what would be required of them.

The project would demand total commitment from everyone from 1 November 1984 to the finish of the race in Portsmouth in May 1986. Those who were selected for the crew were asked to sign a form agreeing to that commitment, so they had to give a lot of thought to devoting the best part of 20 months of their lives, unpaid, to *Lion* before signing on the dotted line. They were also told that they would have to pay all of their own expenses — such as getting to the start if they didn't help sail the boat to England — if fundraising didn't go as well as hoped. Nobody balked at these requirements. I wasn't at all surprised by this. I'd managed to recruit some of the best people in a sailing-mad community. They lived for yachting and most of them had organised themselves into jobs within the yachting industry so that they could tackle their sport on a sort of semi-professional basis. They would be good and they would stick with their task when the going got tough. People who readily made the sorts of commitments that these guys had, would be the types who wouldn't hesitate to get out of their bunks in the middle of a nasty night for a sail change. They would be the types who would be prepared to pump the bilges or get on with the other less attractive jobs on a racing yacht without moaning and groaning.

You can't contemplate a long and demanding race without those sorts of people. Identifying them involves a lot of gut feel and, I suppose, depends on what the skipper is looking for. I can't see any point in racing around the world for seven months with someone you don't like. As it turned out, I could have half-filled the boat again with guys I'd have been happy to go to sea with for a long period. In quite a few cases, those people ended up with *NZI Enterprise,* Digby Taylor's 80ft Farr maxi, which was to become *Lion*'s arch rival in the promotional and fundraising stakes back home. Taylor was looking for a crew later than I was and he ended up with an extremely good group of people too.

Kevin Shoebridge (Shoeby), 21, sailmaker.

Tony Rae (Trae), 23, sailmaker.

Paul MacDonald (Mac D), 22, engineer.

Grant Dalton (Dalts) came to me very early in the piece and asked to be considered not only for the project but also as a watch leader. Dalts was 12th man for the *Ceramco* crew and found himself a berth on *Flyer* when no gap appeared with us. I had no doubts about him as crew for *Lion* but was not sure how he would work out as a watch leader. The two watch-leader positions would be the most critical on the boat and would dictate how efficiently *Lion* was sailed. The watch leader has to encourage the people on his team to keep driving. He has to be on the ball all of the time, always seeking optimum performance from boat and crew. Others can doze off on the weather rail, or under a sail bag in the cockpit when conditions are bleak. But not the watch leader. He has to be constantly alert and enthusiastic. I wasn't sure how Dalts would handle people but decided to give him the chance he was after. There's nothing like being thrown in at the deep end to bring out the best, or the worst, in a man.

My other watch-leader decision rocked everyone. I was surprised when Ross Guiniven (Roscoe) applied for a place on the boat. A former sailmaker, he had done virtually everything else in yachting except a long-distance race. I had my doubts that he would last the journey but he was a dedicated, skilled and enthusiastic yachtsman. After a lot of thought, I decided to give him a real opportunity. I asked him to be my other watch leader. Ross was taken aback by that but said he would give it a go. He was a big success. He was right into the project and the guys in his watch loved him.

Mike Quilter (Mike) joined up originally as one of the sailmakers but later would be elevated to watch leader. He was dead keen to do the project, whatever he was asked to undertake. One of Tom Schnackenberg's key men in *Australia II*'s sails programme for the 1983 assault on the America's Cup, Mike knew what commitment was, and had a wonderfully easy-going nature. He would fit in very well and I was encouraged by the fact that he was so keen to join *Lion*. If this was the calibre of person we were to attract, we were in good shape.

The fact that the Whitbread organisers don't make a doctor compulsory on every boat in the Round the World race is bewildering. I find it even more puzzling that all skippers don't take one anyway. A doctor on board could make the difference

---

Bob Graham (Bob), 22, engineer.

Roy Mason (Roy), 37, engineer.

Glen Sowry (Sweet and Sowry), 22, electrician.

between winning and losing. If, for instance, one of your crew hurts his neck, what do you do without on-board medical advice. Thinking the injury is serious, you'd probably withdraw from the race and seek the closest medical treatment. But you would be throwing your race away for nothing if the injury turned out to be only a temporary problem. A doctor in the crew would give you qualified advice on which to base your decision.

Fraser Maxwell (Doc) was working in the casualty department of Whakatane Hospital when he applied to join *Lion*. It is a regional hospital in a township that services a rural community in the Bay of Plenty, so Fraser was diagnosing and treating the full range of injuries and complaints. He'd done quite a bit of offshore racing, much of it on Peter Spencer's Farr 55 *Cotton Blossom*. I had the chance of a doctor who was also a yachtsman who knew what he was letting himself in for. I snapped him up and he immediately underwent several courses, including one on dentistry, to ensure that he would be able to handle almost any medical problem that came his way.

Simon Gundry (Si) was one of the stalwarts on *Ceramco* and won the personality of the race award in 1981-82. I had asked all of the *Ceramco* crew if they would like to join me on *Lion*. Simon was really keen to do it again and I was delighted to welcome him aboard. A good, strong all-rounder, he was a real organiser and would have a big influence on crew morale.

I couldn't have wished for better than those who made the grade in the sailmaking and trimming department. Grant Spanhake (Fuzz) had helped build *Ceramco*'s sails while working for the Lidgard loft. He had done a lot of offshore racing and came highly recommended by Jim Lidgard, whose opinions I respected. Grant struck me as a little nervous and unsure of himself to begin with, but so are a lot of people when faced with an interview which could affect their future. He wasn't big physically, but he was nimble and fast, and Jim Lidgard assured me there weren't many better trimmers around. Grant would be a good man to have in the crew.

Kevin Shoebridge (Shoeby) had sailed with me on *Lady B* in the 1983 Admiral's Cup. He knew what to expect from me and I was fully aware of his qualities. Fit and strong, he was another sailmaker who lived for yachting. He was also very personable and good with people, which would be quite an asset to the public relations side

---

Godfrey Cray (Goddy), 25, electrician.

Martin Ford (Jaapi), 36, lawyer.

Ed Danby (Pom), 24, rigger.

of the project. I was keen to have him on board.

Tony Rae (Trae) was also involved with *Ceramco's* sails while working for the Lidgard loft. He had applied to join *Ceramco's* crew but was only 19 at the time. I considered that a bit young. This time around he was a mature 23-year-old who was a big and fit triathlete. Practical, with a delightfully dry sense of humour, he was on, provided he recognised exactly what he was getting into.

The same quality of people emerged for the engineering berths. Paul MacDonald (Mac D) was another who had sailed with me on *Lady B* in 1983. Easy going, I had never heard him utter a bad word about anyone. Since the '83 Admiral's Cup he had been racing on maxis such as *Ondine* and *Kialoa,* so he was a must for *Lion.*

Bob Graham (Bob), like Paul, was a qualified engineer who had shelved his career while he indulged in his love of sailing. He was to have joined *Lady B* but there was a last-minute breakdown in communications. Instead, he went off to join the maxi circuit, finishing up on *Ondine.* So he too came highly qualified and was an almost automatic choice.

Roy Mason (Roy) was involved in the building of *Lion* from the outset. He had a lot to do with the aluminium, internal space frame, knew everything about the engineering of the boat, and was fully conversant with the plumbing and the mechanics. I don't think Roy had considered joining the crew, but I thought he would be a good man to have along. Big and strong, he had done a lot of sailing, including the 1983 Admiral's Cup series on *Inca.* He took a couple of days to think it over, then came back with a 'yes'.

I had no problems with electricians either. Glen Sowry (Sweet and Sowry) was a 22-year-old with a quality dinghy background. He was campaigning an Olympic-class 470 when, almost as soon as the *Lion* project was announced, he approached me for a berth. He hadn't done any offshore sailing and I told him I couldn't consider him until he had some blue-water miles under his belt. He responded by joining Don St Clair Brown's 50ft Lexcen design *Anticipation* for the race from New Zealand to Tahiti, and then the Clipper Cup series in Hawaii. On his return, he was quite frank about his being seasick but still wanted to come. I admired his honesty and tenacity and decided to give him his chance. Apart from anything else, he was obviously a class helmsman and we would need a few of those.

Cole Sheehan (BC), 22, chef.

Andy Taylor (Raw Meat), 21, boatbuilder.

Paul von Zalinski (Vonny), 40, boat deliverer.

Godfrey Cray (Goddy) was an unknown to me, even though he had raced the 1981-82 Whitbread on *Outward Bound*. He was one of the last people to apply but he came with good references and was highly spoken of by the people who had already been given the nod for *Lion*. He'd done the race before and knew the commitment required. This tipped the scales in his favour. I was later to find that Goddy was a man of many fine qualities and was never to regret my decision.

The duo which signed on as riggers were both born overseas but qualified for *Lion*'s 'all-Kiwi' line-up because they had assured access to New Zealand passports. Martin Ford (Jaapi) was born in Durban, South Africa. I'd met him briefly when he was on the maxi *Mistress Quickly* and I was on *Condor*. He'd raced practically everywhere in the world on big and small boats so was one of the most experienced people to apply. He was also a keen rigger, so was doubly valuable. Relaxed and humorous, he wanted to do the Whitbread with us for all the right reasons. Married to a New Zealand woman, Ginny, he had been living in Auckland for some time and would have no trouble getting a Kiwi passport.

Ed Danby (Pom) was born in England but his family background was very much New Zealand. I first met him on a cold December day in Southampton when I was invited for a sail on the J-class *Valsheda*. He was soon to leave for Auckland and I suggested he could find himself a job on the *Lion* boatbuilding team. A top rigger who had been involved in two British challenges for the America's Cup (even though he was only 24), Ed fitted easily into Tim Gurr's team and, when I asked him to apply for a crew position, he jumped at the chance.

In the specialist departments, this left a cook and a boatbuilder to unearth. Simon helped take care of the cook problem. I'd received one application, from a Northland woman who had only dinghy experience but who sounded an excellent proposition. I was about to accept her when Simon introduced me to Cole Sheehan (BC). Cole also had a limited sailing background, but he was a qualified chef and had the full backing of his family in applying to join *Lion*. Simon was a close friend of that family and I knew that he would make sure that Cole performed.

With a crew of 22, most of them big guys with big appetites, he would have to produce good meals quickly, working almost predominantly with freeze-dried foods.

Ralph Lucas (Ralph), 28, physed teacher.

Graeme Handley (Balls), 23, yacht deliverer.

Aran Hansen (Whale), 25, drainage contractor.

He would also have to bake fresh bread and scones to vary the diet and titillate taste buds. To help him achieve this, we were installing an all-electric galley in *Lion* with a full-size domestic range, and two microwave-convection ovens.

When boatbuilder Andy Taylor (Raw Meat) applied for a berth, it was as a general hand. Still serving his apprenticeship with McMullen & Wing, he was big and naturally very strong. He would be excellent around the mast, where he preferred to work, or on the grinders. But I had my full complement and, reluctantly, had to turn him down. Not too long afterwards, John Newton decided he had to put business before sailing and withdrew. When I phoned Andy to see if he still wanted to come, 'too right' was the reply.

In the general hand category, I had signed a nice mix of talent, youth and experience. Paul von Zalinski (Vonny) was the cook on *Ceramco*. I wrote to him as soon as I knew the *Lion* project was on, and asked him 'how about coming again?' I told him he could come as the cook if he liked, or as deck crew. He accepted a deck crew role immediately. I'm sure he didn't tell his wife Stef what he was going to do until much later on. Vonny was an invaluable person to have around on *Ceramco*. He was the butt for a lot of humour, but he gave as much as he got. It would be good to have his company and experience again.

Ralph Lucas (Ralph) was a physical education teacher who was another Jim Lidgard recommendation. He'd raced the 1984 Clipper Cup on Alistair Shanks' Lidgard 50-footer *Black Sheep,* and then had moved on to America to extend his sailing experience. A fairly quiet sort, without being at all introverted, he was strong and a good all-rounder who was favourably regarded by the peer group that was already confirmed crew. His strength would be an asset in a number of positions on *Lion*.

Graeme Handley (Balls) was a stranger to me. He was introduced by Grant Dalton and was friendly with a number of the other guys who'd already been accepted. The paid hand on Tim Sneddon's Ross design *Blast Furnace,* he was really keen to join *Lion* and, at 23, was another young man who lived for his yachting. Graeme was a little unsure of himself, not certain what he could or couldn't do, but I was fairly confident he would work out.

The final member of the line-up was to have been former North Shore rugby player Grant Davidson, a powerful sort who had done a lot of miles on maxis like *Condor.* He was working in Fremantle but I knew his qualifications well enough to approve his application. Grant was to return to New Zealand to join the project just before *Lion* was launched. He withdrew at the 11th hour and I was left with one berth to fill.

By that stage Aran Hansen (Whale) was back from a Soling campaign, with Tom Dodson and Simon Daubney, at the Los Angeles Olympics. He was matey with quite a few of the *Lion* crew and was extremely willing to lend a hand with the jobs that had to be done to prepare *Lion* for her launch, without ever indicating to me that he was interested in joining the team. When Grant Davidson pulled out, I asked Dalts if Aran might like to be the replacement. Dalts told me Aran would love to, but was too timid to ask. I had a chat with him the following day and he was in. He had no ocean-racing experience, but as one of New Zealand's top dinghy people, he obviously had talent and, through his Olympic effort, knew all about commitment. Because of his sheer size — 6ft 3ins and 20 stone — he would be very good at a number of jobs on the boat.

By this stage, late September 1984, *Lion* was having the finishing touches applied by the Gurr team, Tom Clark had completed his sponsorship package and had a national fundraising drive under way for campaign costs, and I had a crew which I regarded as potentially the best in Whitbread race history.

3. The Going Gets Tough

Lion New Zealand, looking resplendent with her metallic silver paint job, made quite a sight as she was trucked over the Auckland Harbour Bridge a few days before the launch date. With a traffic department escort, she was manoeuvred through a carefully selected route from her Poland Road shed, through Birkenhead and Northcote, over the bridge and through Ponsonby to the McMullen & Wing hardstand at Westhaven. The only problems were with occasional overhead wires but, these apart, the big move went without a hitch. It would take a couple of days to fit and fair the keel so everything was on schedule for the Sunday, November 4 debut.

If *Lion* looked good from the outside, she was somewhat sensational down below. Rather than follow tradition and have a boat designer produce the accommodation layout, we had commissioned commercial design consultants Bruce Woods and Bret de Thier to come up with something more in keeping with the high-tech nature of the *Lion* campaign. They produced an interior which was superbly practical while also futuristic in its concept and colour scheming. Maxis are, by their very nature, big boats. But when you start cramming aboard all of the equipment they need, particularly for a race like the Whitbread, you quickly begin to run out of space, especially when you need to keep the ends of the boat as light as possible to obviate pitching in a seaway.

The navigatorium resembled the cockpit of a Boeing 747 or a DC-10, bristling with sophisticated electronics which were neatly arranged within reach of the navigator's aircraft-type seat. The navigational and tactical aspects of the 1985-86 Whitbread were going to be even more critical than usual with the prospect of six maxis match-racing around the world. It made sense to ensure that the person doing navigation and tactics — in *Lion*'s case it would be me — was comfortable in an environment in which he would spend the greater part of every day at sea.

If the navigatorium attracted immediate attention, so did the galley. Tucked away towards the stern of the boat, it too was compact and packed with equipment. But again it was absolutely functional with everything cleverly located to make the chef's job as easy as possible. The decision to have an all-electric galley raised a few eyebrows. The more traditional fuel sources on offshore racing boats are bottled gas or kerosene.

The more I thought about it, however, the more sense electric equipment made. The alternative was gas, and *Lion* would have to carry a lot of it to cater for 22 guys for five or six weeks at a time. Gas bottles have to be stowed in lockers which drain to the outside for safety reasons. That meant, theoretically, on deck so it would be a fair bit of weight up high.

An all-electric galley would use up a lot of power too. But the race rules required us to have a separate generator and, with *Lion*'s communications and desalination plant requirements, it would have to be a good one. If we were going to generate that much power anyway, why not hook the galley into the same system? The slight amount of extra fuel to facilitate this would be in the diesel tanks, down low in the boat in the ideal location. From there, it was a short step to normal household range and kettles and microwave-convection ovens. A qualified chef, and in Cole Sheehan we had such a person, would be able to work wonders down there.

The risk was power failure, but if the generator faltered we would have a back-up 240-volt supply from the main engine. If that failed too, and that would be highly unusual, we would carry one gas bottle to fuel an emergency single-burner stove. With careful use, we could get a few meals out of that set-up. We had to consider

The navigatorium, bristling with electronic wizardry.

The main hatch entry with drinks lockers on the port side.

what to do at night when the on-deck watch wanted hot drinks or soup. We didn't want to be starting up the generator for those requirements. The solution was a set of eight specially made stainless steel thermos flasks which would keep water close to boiling point for up to 13 hours. They were unbreakable with highly secure screw-on lids so that there was no risk of someone getting scalded in the event of a knockdown with gear flying all over the place.

The desalination unit would be capable of making 6000 litres of fresh water a day. That would be more than enough for domestic purposes so the two toilet capsules — one near the mast and the other tucked in on the port side aft — were equipped with showers. The Whitbread wasn't going to be a pleasure cruise for the Lion crew, but the capacity to provide for them, with no extra weight involved, a couple of quick, fresh-water showers a week (hot or cold) would make an enormous difference to crew morale.

The big day dawned with everything ready for a major launching occasion at Princes Wharf, Auckland's passenger ship terminal which would be the centre of activities when the Whitbread fleet reached New Zealand in January 1986. Not taking any chances, we slipped Lion into the water from the McMullen & Wing travel-lift at first light — just to make sure everything was as it should be — before loading her on to the Auckland Harbour Board's heavy-lift crane for the short journey by water around to the passenger terminal.

The launch itself was one of those occasions for which Auckland was becoming famous. Thousands of people turned out, afloat and ashore, to see New Zealand's first full-on maxi make her debut. Lady Tait, wife of Admiral Sir Gordon Tait, patron of the New Zealand International Yacht Racing Trust, broke the traditional bottle of bubbly across Lion's bow to launch the campaign proper and the city celebrated in grand fashion. Tom Clark and his team, which included Alan Topham, who played such a major part in the Ceramco exercise, Michael Clark, Jock O'Connor, and accountant John Balgarnie who, as Tom put it, made sure there were 'no holes in the bottom of the fundraising bucket', could relax a little. They'd delivered. With the support of an influential group of sponsors, they'd provided me with a boat which had the pedigree, the constructional integrity and the equipment to win the Whitbread.

Hanging locker aft of the mast and nothing forward.

Compact and well thought out galley, microwaves and all.

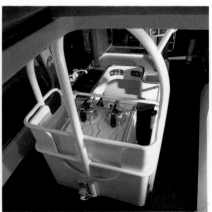

Lion is escorted off Auckland Harbour Bridge on her way to her launch.

Alan Topham

John Balgarnie

Tom Clark, with invited dignitaries and main sponsors, addresses the thousands who turned up for *Lion*'s launching.

John Andrew Ford
Mogal Corporation

AIR NEW ZE   ATLAS CORP·A
Mike Clark

The formalities over, *Lion* is lowered into the water for her first dip.

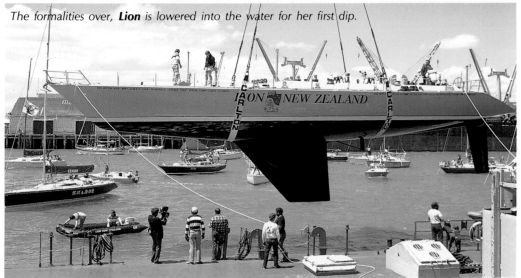

Now my job, and that of the crew, began in earnest. We had one short month in which to bring *Lion* up to scratch for the Sydney-Hobart race and much of that month would be taken up with three or four cruises a day to introduce the sponsors and major contributors to the boat that they'd made possible. It was an exhausting schedule and we were all relieved when the time came to cast off from our berth on a permanent barge at Captain Cook Wharf and head for the Tasman Sea and Sydney. It was blowing fresh from the north-east as we slipped our lines, yet there was a huge crowd, braving a miserable evening, to see us go. On board we had several guests, including Tom, and the full crew who were looking forward to letting *Lion* loose in the ocean.

The 1300-mile crossing was uneventful except for a real blow a couple of days off the New South Wales coast. *Lion* was reefed down to her smallest gear in 50 knots of breeze but still jumping out of big waves. We slowed her down and then hove to. There was no point risking damage or injury with everyone so new to the yacht. That little dust-up was a portent of things to come in the 1984 Sydney-Hobart classic, but in that one there would be no easing back when the going got tough.

The 630-mile Hobart race is one of the most famous of all offshore events. Given mass media coverage, it is a sporting institution in Australia along with events like the Melbourne Cup horse race and the Aussie Rules football grand final. The course, on paper, looks simple enough — more of a coastal race than a blue-water classic. It involves a hard right turn at Sydney Heads, down the New South Wales coast and across Bass Strait on to the eastern coastline of Tasmania. Another hard right turn, this time at Tasman Island, across Storm Bay and a short sprint up the Derwent River to the finish off Hobart's Wrest Point Casino. No problems.

But the simplicity of the track belies the difficulty it can present when the elements are unfavourable. The New South Wales coast, with its unpredictable currents, can be rugged enough when it is blowing hard from the southern quarter. Bass Strait can be something else again, a funnel for winds and currents as the Indian Ocean squeezes through between mainland Australia and Tasmania to enter the Tasman Sea. The Aussies call Bass Strait 'The Paddock'. More often than not it is a deeply ploughed field.

The coast of Tasmania is tactically tricky, but frequently the best, or worst, is yet to come. Tasman Island is one of the great maritime landmarks although it is further off the beaten path of the great trade routes than, say, the Cape of Good Hope and Cape Horn. It juts out from the southern tip of the Tasman Peninsula, its stark cliffs sculpted into memorable designs and shapes by centuries of winds and seas conjured up in the Antarctic, not that far to the south.

Tasman Island marks the turn into the aptly named Storm Bay where many a good yacht's race has come unstuck. Then there's the Derwent. It can be blowing old boots 'outside' yet be as calm as a millpond in the river. There are generations of yachtsmen with good reason to wish that the Hobart race finish was off the Iron Pot, at the mouth of the Derwent, rather than 10 miles upstream off the city of Hobart itself.

One of the greatest hazards of the race, however, is the start. In days gone by, with smaller fleets, a start-line within the confines of Sydney Harbour, off Shark Island to be precise, was an admirable idea, opening proceedings within a stone's throw of the magnificent harbour shoreline so that the public could get a good view of the action and, down the years, develop a real fervour for the race. The same approach held good with the advent of television so that live coverage became a feature of the Boxing Day departure and increased the audience, and the interest, immeasurably. But in recent years, with the enormous development in yachting, the Hobart race has grown out of all proportions. The 150-boat fleets in the congested start area, and then the crowded 'fairway' to the Heads and the open sea, make for scenes more appropriate to stock car circuits.

The line-up for the 1984 classic comprised 152 boats. Among them were the 79ft Holland design *Condor*, one of the stars of the maxi circuit, the 76ft Lexcen design *Apollo*, revamped yet again, the much-changed 80ft Frers design *Ragamuffin*, and the 77ft Tasker design *Vengeance*. All four were previous line honours winners of the race — *Condor* in 1983, *Apollo* in 1978, *Ragamuffin* (as *Bumblebee IV*) in 1979, and *Vengeance* in 1981. They would provide a valuable yardstick to *Lion*'s potential.

We had some more PR obligations to take care of in the week before the start but generally were able to wind down after the hectic pace of getting the boat ready and then bringing her across the Tasman. Christmas Day was delightful. Pippa's parents, John and Judy Glanville, were over from Britain for the start and joined us on *Lion* for a festive cruise down harbour to Quarantine Bay, in the lee of Sydney's North Head, for Christmas lunch. It was a very convivial scene, despite the fact that nobody was partaking of alcoholic beverage to any degree with the race now less than 24 hours away. Proceedings were orderly until a dinghy hove into sight with three people aboard. The male rowing the boat was calling 'Good on yer Kiwis' and clearly was intent on joining us for a drink. The crew had no objections to that for his two companions were rather voluptuous ladies wearing only bikini bottoms. Topless females are somewhat passé in Sydney but the sight of these two running around the deck of *Lion* with next to nothing on was almost too much for a group of Simon's Californian friends — including the somewhat notorious Gary 'Weasel' King — and we politely had to get rid of our 'guests' on the pretext that we were upping anchor to return to the Cruising Yacht Club of Australia in Rushcutters Bay.

Boxing Day dawned brilliantly fine and the harbour was already crowded with spectator boats as, at 1000 hours, we slipped our lines and motored the two miles to the start area. The wind was from the south and freshening. It was going to be a tight reach down the harbour before hardening up through the Heads for a beat down the New South Wales coast. No doubt there would be a real jam at the windward end of the line which would be a good place to stay away from.

Pippa did the 1980 Hobart with us on *Ceramco* but this time had to stay ashore with Sarah-Jane. She felt a bit left out of things as a result, but later was to be rather glad she didn't come. *Lion* was racing with her full complement of 22, plus Tom Clark, radio commentator Pete Montgomery and film-maker John Toon who was shooting 35mm footage for a *Lion* special which was to be shown in cinemas throughout New Zealand. Both Tom and Pete did the race on *Ceramco* too, so it was a bit like old times as the 10-minute gun went and we got down to business.

I went for a conservative start from the middle of the line, not wishing to push my luck in such traffic. *Condor* was down the leeward end looking to make good time in clear air on the northern side of the harbour before hardening up to fetch through the Heads. *Apollo* was down there with her but the other big boats were towards the windward end and out quickly. Weaving our way through the congestion, we gradually worked *Lion* into a windward position and, as the wind freed and lifted us slightly, tried a spinnaker. It was a flat-cut, heavy-air kite and for a while did us proud. But we had problems keeping it set as the wind swung and headed us.

Lion in the thick of the charge down Sydney Harbour.

Never mind, we were there to learn what made *Lion* and her wardrobe tick.

Condor had looked sad down to leeward, but not as sad as *Apollo* which broached out violently when she tried a kite to answer the wind change. On Bob Bell's *Condor*, they ignored the temptation of a spinnaker and lifted up into the Heads at full speed under a big genoa. It was the smart way to go and *Condor's* reward was the honour of being first out into the Tasman. *Apollo* and *Ragamuffin* were next followed by the 66ft Joe Adams design *Spirit of Queensland* which, as *Helsal II*, gave *Ceramco* such a good race in 1980. Then came *Lion*, *Vengeance* and the new Frers 66-footer *Freight Train*. *Lion* was fifth to emerge. We were reasonably happy with that as we hauled on the gear, on starboard tack, and laid along the cliffs off Sydney's southern shoreline into a sea that was already large and lumpy as well as churned white by the hundreds of launches and runabouts that were determined to get a close look at the maxis before having to turn back to shelter.

The forecast from the race office that morning had not been promising. Gale-force south-westerlies were predicted later in the day and, as we started into the long punch south, the signs were that the weatherman had it dead right. For the moment though we had more to worry about. It was no use trying to climb through to windward of *Condor*, *Ragamuffin* and *Apollo* as we chased them down the coast, so we drove off through to leeward of them. The first time we tacked back into the coast to regain some windward ground, we were ahead of everyone, feeling rather pleased with ourselves and with our brand new, untried machine. But then the wind increased and the sea condition changed, and we dropped out of gear. *Condor* piled time on us and *Ragamuffin* eased ahead. *Apollo* wasn't a problem. We'd gone through her lee like she was anchored and now, with headsail problems, she was a long way astern.

Not knowing the sail combinations that *Lion* would like, we were struggling against maxis whose performances were well documented and whose crews knew how to extract those performances. Thus far we'd been using a No. 4 headsail and full main which was the norm for *Kialoa* and *Condor* in the 25-knot winds we were punching. But for some reason, now that the wind was up, we were getting dropped off. We tried everything with that combination but with no real improvement. *Lion* wouldn't point. So we changed up to the No. 3 headsail and slapped a reef into the main — and bingo! *Lion* took off and within one and a half hours we went from a mile behind *Ragamuffin* to a mile ahead, straight out to windward and going faster. The boat was feeling really good and we started to wind in *Condor*.

By now the gale was building. We beat on into the night not knowing that the first casualties were already on their way back to Sydney or seeking help, or that in the next 36 hours the fleet would be decimated. The first indications that this would be a war of attrition between the elements and the fleet came the next morning. *Condor* was out of the race, her steering gear wrecked when a turning block tore away from the hull. She was limping back to Sydney in difficult seas. She was only one of 31 yachts in trouble, however. Four boats had been dismasted during the night. The other 27 reported varying problems from critical rig or hull damage to chronic seasickness. *Ragamuffin* and *Apollo* were also among the retired. *Ragamuffin* had broken her main boom gooseneck fitting and had a seriously injured crewman. *Apollo* had blown most of her sails and also had injured crew.

As we listened to these reports, *Lion* was off Batemans Bay, working the rhumbline course some 20 miles off the coast. She'd covered 110 miles in the first 17 hours of the race and was the only big boat without problems. In fact she was, with the exception of *Vengeance*, the only big boat left in the race. We had some seasickness on board, but that was all. Back on shore, race officials at the CYCA were clearly worried about the situation. The previous record retirement total in a Hobart race was 57 (of 127 boats) in 1977. This year's fleet hadn't been at sea for 24 hours, yet the casualty list was high and growing by the hour.

By now the wind was gusting 45 knots from the SSW and *Lion* had almost dealt a permanent blow to the well-known voice of Pete Montgomery. He'd been trying to get some sleep lying on the floor alongside the navigatorium when the boat jumped out of a wave and hurled my brass parallel rulers off the nav table. They caught Pete fair in the throat and dug in. He was okay, thinking he'd only received a knock, until blood started to run down his chest. Startled and not knowing the extent of the injury, he quickly sought Doc Fraser who was comatose in his bunk with a rather severe case of mal de mer. Pete was somewhat perturbed when the only response he got from the Doc was: 'Yes, you've cut your throat.' The Doc promptly rolled over to nurse his own problem.

Seeking assistance, Pete came to me. He again struck out because I was lacking sleep after a night of plotting *Lion* through the gale and keeping an eye on proceedings. As a result, my bedside manner was about as subtle as that of the ailing doctor. I sought advice from the Doc who told me to close the cut with strips of plaster, spray the wound with antiseptic, and then cover the whole thing with a coating of spray-on plastic skin. I did all of this — the sprays sending Pete through the cabin top — only to find that I'd used the backing strips off the plasters instead of the plasters themselves. The whole process had to be repeated — this time by the real doctor.

Later that afternoon the race office issued a radio alert for a 15-foot-diameter steel oil rig buoy which had broken loose in Bass Strait and was being blown into the path of the fleet. By the evening the casualty list had reached 70 and late that night we were numbed by the news that 70-year-old Wally Russell had been lost overboard from the 38ft Hank Kaufman design *Yahoo II*. Three huge waves had swept over the yacht, capsizing it and washing Russell, a veteran of 15 previous Hobart races, over the side. The yacht was on its ear, completely engulfed by water. When she righted herself, Russell was 30 metres away waving to attract attention. His crewmates frantically started the engine which ran for only 10 seconds before cutting out. It took two minutes to manoeuvre *Yahoo II* back to Russell's position. By then he was face down in the water and drifting away from help. *Yahoo II*'s crew risked their own lives trying to find Russell again but finally had to look to their own safety in huge seas and headed for shelter in Jervis Bay.

The fleet's radio relay ship, the former Port Phillip Bay pilot vessel *Wyuna*, was diverted to the area to take over the search. She was joined at dawn the next day by three aircraft. But the operation had to be scaled down and then abandoned when conditions deteriorated and the chances of finding Russell alive became nil. The Hobart race had claimed its first victim in its 39-year history. Deputy race officer Gordon Marshall issued a warning to yachts still racing. It read: 'In the light of forecasts please assess the ability of your boat and crew in proceeding across Bass Strait. A conscious decision should be made on each yacht before continuing across.' By 0700 hours the next day the casualty list was 78 boats and the barometer was dropping again. The forecast was for south to south-west winds of 30-40 knots with very rough seas.

A further 53 miles down the track than anyone else and entering Bass Strait,

Kite reaching for Tasman Island, 100 miles ahead of the opposition.

the *Lion* crew could vouch for the accuracy of the weatherman's predictions. We were taking quite a hammering and had been beating for 41 hours to cover 270 miles since the start on Boxing Day. The fact that we were leading on the water and on handicap, and that we might be poised to repeat *Ceramco*'s historic line and handicap double, was incentive enough to keep us driving despite the heavy going. We didn't need to nurse *Lion*. She was handling it well even though she was as wet as a half-tide rock and was falling off some big ones. Pete Montgomery, his neck wound now taken care of, told listeners back in New Zealand that it was 'like driving a 10-ton truck off the top of a three-storey building, every couple of minutes'.

While we didn't need to nurse *Lion*, it was prudent to hold her back a bit. You can't keep dropping a big boat off 25 and 30-foot seas all the time without doing some damage, no matter how strong your boat is. Anyway, we didn't need to push to or past the limits. All the big competition had gone. We were on our own and doing fine.

By 0600 hours the following morning, after nearly three days of the race, the retirement total was 101 boats, and as far as could be ascertained only 36 of the survivors were still racing. The rest were sheltering in ports on the southern New South Wales coast, waiting for the weather to abate before continuing. The weatherman was still forecasting south to south-west winds of 30-40 knots, but in Bass Strait it had swung to the south-east and was beginning to drop. *Lion* was starting to ease away down the eastern coast of Tasmania having averaged 10 knots overnight to cover 150 miles in 15 hours.

With 170 miles still to go, we were averaging nine knots in flatter water. It had been a slow first half of the race and it now looked like being a fast finish. This would favour the smaller boats and we were now facing an uphill struggle to save our time on handicap. Our closest rival on the water was *Vengeance*, 95 miles astern. She'd been reduced to a reefed mainsail only at the height of the gale. The pressure for handicap honours was coming from the 40ft Farr design *Indian Pacific* which had gone well out to sea, to the east of the rhumbline the first night out, and had experienced little of the punishment that had been meted out closer inshore. In addition to this, she had been lifted on starboard tack going out, had found more southerly current to push her down the course, and, when 108 miles off the coast, clocked into a south-easterly. She tacked on the change as she entered Bass Strait and was rocketing towards Tasman Island with a breeze that had kept shifting through to the north-east.

It was cold comfort to me that I'd recognised the same possibilities when checking the weather maps on Christmas Day, but *Lion* would need to cover the other big boats closer inshore. We closed on Tasman Island almost 3 days 6 hours into the race, still the handicap leader and with a gap of 100 miles between us and *Vengeance*. We might still get the double, but something would have to happen to slow down the smaller boats which were on the Tasmanian coast with fresh tailwinds.

The 8-10 knot north-easterly bringing us in towards Storm Bay became a 30-knot north-easter, sucked in at greater velocity by the high cliffs on Tasmania's southern shore. We averaged 13 knots with the wind on the beam, and then hardened up for the approach to the Derwent. The final 10 miles were mostly a drift in light headwinds and we didn't cross the line until 0030 hours.

In her first competitive outing, *Lion* had really been put to the test and she had come through with flying colours. The welcome she received was exceptional, even

Constitution Dock in the small hours — time for a team Steinlager.

by Hobart standards. The gales and the mounting casualty list had been given headline treatment by the Australian media and now it seemed everyone in Hobart wanted to see the first boat that had survived all the drama. *Lion* was almost engulfed by spectator craft for the slow, drifting, last few miles in the Derwent. She was lit up by television lights from waterline to masthead. There was a traditional jazz band on a ferry to accompany our progress and constant runabouts zooming in and out of the darkness to shout congratulations. By the time we reached our berth outside Constitution Dock, the shore was wall-to-wall people. Fortunately, we had grabbed Pippa and Sarah-Jane aboard from a big catamaran minutes after crossing the line. They would never have reached *Lion* had they tackled the job from the shore.

We had taken 3 days 11 hours 31 minutes 21 seconds for the 630-mile journey. This was well outside *Kialoa*'s 1975 record of 2 days 14 hours 36 minutes 56 seconds and 16 hours 45 minutes slower than *Ceramco*'s winning time in 1980. But you couldn't compare the performances in those terms. This had proved the toughest Hobart on record with only 46 of the 152 starters reaching Hobart, an attrition rate of 70 percent. *Kialoa* and *Ceramco* had enjoyed downwind slides. *Lion* had punched into 40-knot winds and big seas for the best part of three days before the wind swung enough for her to ease sheets and start to wriggle. We missed the double. The small boats came in fast to dominate the major placings, *Indian Pacific* doing particularly well to win on handicap.

But we were first to finish by 12½ hours, which represented a lead of more than 100 miles, and we proved the boat's potential and her ability to withstand conditions which, although they had destroyed this Hobart fleet, could be the norm for much longer periods in the Whitbread.

We were pleased enough with all of that as, six days later, we headed back down the Derwent and into Storm Bay for a dash back across the Tasman to Milford Sound — the Hall of the Mountain King in an impressive fiord on the west coast of the South Island of New Zealand. From here, after a couple of days' rest and recreation, we would embark on a 14-port tour of the country to fly the flag, show the people of New Zealand what we hoped was a Whitbread winner and raise money to pay for *Lion*'s Round the World race campaign.

That tour surprised even those of us who had done a smaller version of the same exercise with *Ceramco*. The scene was set in Bluff, the southernmost tip of the 'mainland' South Island where the queues of people lined up to see through the boat were several hundred metres long despite cold, rainy weather. It was much the same everywhere we went — the hospitality and generosity were almost overwhelming. In the space of just over three weeks more than 40,000 people were shown through the boat, parting with in excess of $300,000 for the tour and acquiring a whole range of *Lion* souvenirs.

It was tough on the crew but in the tougher months to come, maybe in the middle of a bad night in the Southern Ocean, they would remember the little old ladies from the country areas of New Zealand who travelled far and handed over hard-earned dollars just to see what these young fellas from Auckland were up to this time and to do their bit to help. Pride and patriotism had been invaluable on *Ceramco* when her mast came down. The *Lion* crew would have even greater reason to invoke those qualities should they be needed.

Milford Sound — The Hall of the Mountain King.

And does it not seem hard to you,
when all the sky is clear and blue,
and I should like so much to play,
to have to go to bed by day?
Robert Louis Stevenson
Bed In Summer

4. And Baby Comes Too

Sunday, 14 April 1985: Time for *Lion* to leave on her delivery voyage to Britain. The hectic first phase of the programme was completed. Fundraising would continue at best speed, but the racing schedules were put on hold until mid-July by which time the crew would have reassembled in England and *Lion* would be based at the Port Hamble marina, near the Solent.

Only five of the racing crew would do the delivery trip — Mike Quilter, Doc Maxwell, Bob Graham, Martin Ford and Cole Sheehan. The others would go back to work for a couple of months before heading individually to the Hamble. Pippa would be making the 13,000-mile voyage, however, as would our now nearly two-year-old daughter Sarah-Jane. Jaapi's wife, Ginny, a registered nurse, would also be with us all the way, as well as Chris Edwards, known as 'the Major' and a good friend of mine from Whitbread races on *Burton Cutter* and *Condor of Bermuda*.

The rest of the ship's complement would be made up of sponsor representatives and special guests, with changes at every stop. On board for the first leg, from Auckland to Easter Island, were Tom Partridge, a well-known Auckland yachtie who was now a New Zealand Line shipmaster, Dick Webster, the recently retired manager of the New Zealand Line, Alan Pellowe, a cheerful sort from Te Kuiti who was representing Epiglass, and Andrew Troupe, who was the winner of a nationwide competition through Lion hotels for which the prize was a trip on *Lion* to Easter Island. The racing crew we left behind reckoned that second prize in the competition was a trip on *Lion* to Panama while third prize was the full deal, all the way to Britain.

The stores had been piling up all the previous week in the Marsden Wharf shed loaned to us by the Auckland Harbour Board. Pippa and Ginny had the job of sorting what would go on *Lion* for the delivery and what had to be loaded into one of two containers, provided by the New Zealand Line (then the Shipping Corporation of New Zealand) to be forwarded to Britain, and then organised into supplies for the race. Most of the staggering mountain of food had been donated by New Zealand companies. Pippa and Ginny were glad of the help of Tom (Partridge) and Dick (Webster) as they packed the delivery-trip requirements in plastic bags and stowed them on board while carefully logging everything that went into the container for legs 1, 2 and 4 of the Whitbread. The log would, we hoped, ensure that we could readily locate items when we came to provision *Lion* in England and repack the container which would go ahead of the boat to Cape Town and then on to Punta del Este. Logistics such as these were now an important part of a Whitbread campaign. The second container which would accompany the food would be chock full of all the spares and equipment that would be needed to keep *Lion* fully operational as a racing machine.

Some of the most important items loaded aboard just before departure were 700 disposable nappies. Sarah-Jane would need some assistance while she underwent

Leaving Auckland Harbour with the non-delivery crew members out in force to see us go.

a maritime version of potty training. The wharf was jammed with people when it came time to cast off. The usual last-minute items were brought aboard — lemons and fresh bread. Then there were several little numbers that were special to *Lion* for this particular journey — a potty trainer and seat, much to the crowd's amusement, a blackboard, a washing machine and a blender, the last for making banana daiquiris.

The send-off party at the Royal New Zealand Yacht Squadron on the Sunday afternoon was an eye-opener. It seemed everyone who had had something to do with the project, plus a lot more besides, were there to bid us farewell. But even that didn't prepare us for the overwhelming numbers out on the Waitemata Harbour and lining the vantage points ashore as we eventually set out. We made our way up harbour to the bridge and set sail under reefed main and big headsail in salute to the Squadron and those who had come to see us off.

Once past Rangitoto Light and headed into the Hauraki Gulf, we took another reef in the main and replaced the big genoa with a No. 5 jib. Ray and Di Walker's impressive motor yacht *Dionysus* was the last of the spectator craft to turn for home. She had my parents, Joyce and Brian, aboard along with Tom Clark, Doug Myers and a lot of our friends. With *Dionysus* went another large vessel on which were the *Lion* racing crew who weren't making the delivery. The next time we saw Rangitoto Light would be in eight months' time when we would come racing in from the Tasman, leading the Whitbread fleet into our home port, with a bit of luck.

With *Lion* making good speed under cruising rig, Sarah-Jane quickly settled down to a game of cards, innocently oblivious of the occasion, which augured well. Then the forecasted bad weather set in, with fresh easterlies churning the gulf into an unusually rough piece of water. Conditions deteriorated rapidly and by the time we approached Colville Channel, between the mainland tip of the Coromandel Peninsula and Great Barrier Island, I was thinking of putting in to Tryphena Harbour for the night. The last few days had been hectic and a good sleep would not go amiss. As if on cue, the generator suddenly stopped and a Tryphena stop became obligatory. There was no point setting out across the South Pacific Ocean with a dud power unit, even if it meant a few red faces when word got out that the much-vaunted round the world racer had made it only as far as Great Barrier after such an emotional send-off.

It took several days to sort out the generator problem and we shifted from Tryphena to Mansion House Bay, on Kawau Island, to make it easier for Ken Lusty to fly in, by Sea Bee Air amphibian, the various experts and parts needed to rectify the fault. So it was on Thursday, April 18 that we finally set out for Easter Island. It had been blowing hard ever since Sunday night and there was a heavy sea running as we beat towards Cuvier Island in 30-knot winds and driving rain squalls, *Lion* snugged down under a fully reefed main and storm jib.

The next few days merged into an unmemorable sequence of heavy seas and grey skies with the boat sopping wet. Sarah-Jane(SJB) was sick for a while and Pippa was feeling quite awful too. What depressing weather in which to depart the New Zealand coast! I had been getting very little sleep so on Sunday, April 21, with a vigorous front forecasted to pass over the top of us in the night, we hove to under trisail only.

The Major was on watch when I went on deck after dinner, the deck floodlight illuminating an already eerie scene. The Major was huddled in the aft steering cockpit, both wheels lashed, with a screaming wind sending solid walls of spray over the entire yacht. No wonder SJB and Pippa weren't feeling the best. We'd rigged a swing in the 'saloon', near the mast, for SJB, using a bosun's chair. This helped take her mind

Mansion House Bay, Kawau, with the Sea Bee Air amphibian bringing in replacement parts.

off things and she came to cheerfully ignore the wildly gyrating environment in which she was now living, swinging about merrily with the boat doing all the work.

By the morning the front had gone through and, at last, we had blue skies with a south-westerly blowing. The seas were still lumpy but the motion, for the first time since leaving Kawau, was bearable, and everyone was feeling human again with albatrosses and sooty shearwaters joining us for this part of the journey. Ginny and Jaapi were on galley duty when we caught a good-sized tuna, much to the delight of SJB, so lunch was a delectable course of fresh fish fried in breadcrumbs with lemon and tomato.

The calmer weather gave us the opportunity to clean the boat below and do some washing. SJB had opened some of her 'rough weather' presents — a tea set, a stamp set, cutting-out scissors and a pile of books — which kept her preoccupied while all the work was being done. We'd decided that it would be very necessary to keep SJB amused at all times during the long voyage, so Pippa had put aboard enough 'presents' to last the distance, even if SJB opened one a day. The idea proved a great success.

Tom Partridge, a veteran passage-maker and an admirable keeper of logs, had developed a badly swollen left big toe which was so painful he was having difficulty sleeping. His record of Doc Maxwell's first official business of the trip observed: 'In what might be called a cockpit consultation, I brought my problem to the notice of the doctor who prodded the toe with his finger a couple of times and concluded that it was broken. Not much in the way of treatment was possible except to give me some sleeping pills. The toe would have to heal itself but at least I would get some decent rest.

'The next day, however, after another sleepless night despite the pills, the toe was worse than ever. The Doc made a second examination, straightened up and turned away to consider his prognosis. At just that moment the boat lurched and the good doctor slipped. The heel of his seaboot, propelled by his full weight, landed fair on the aforementioned big toe. This brought about a spasm of white-hot agony and some unprintable comments from myself.

'But, from that moment on, the swelling and the pain began to reduce rapidly and within three days I was back to normal.'

Doc Maxwell's methods of treatment were somewhat unusual but they appeared to work. He did not escape some constant ribbing, however. The subject of 'unconventional treatment' was a favourite for some time to come and anyone with an ailment, no matter how minor, was told to 'go and get the Doc to stamp on it'.

We were settling down nicely to shipboard life and the meals, as usual, varied according to who was on galley duty and using the microwaves. Several old favourites surfaced, such as 'Root McGoory Stew' which Vonny first perfected on *Ceramco*. Then there were newer dishes such as 'Eggs Whakatane Hospital', 'Microwaved Yuk' and 'Banana Fish Pie Leftovers'.

By April 23 we had reached the most southerly point on our course to Easter Island. At 43 degrees 25 minutes South and 1000 miles out from Auckland, all was well aboard the good ship *Lion*. Tom and the Doc, on ukelele and guitar respectively, provided the entertainment and helped considerably with the task of getting SJB to bed in the evenings. The washing machine that Ray and Di Walker had given us for the voyage was proving a real boon. It didn't take long for clothes to dry on deck after a fast spin.

Tom Partridge takes the helm while the Blakes enjoy a family chat.

The Major had started mixing some lethal cocktails for 'happy hour' and to celebrate his birthday on April 26, he organised a gambling gala. A pontoon school started immediately after breakfast and lasted until late afternoon when the manager of the casino finally succumbed to an overdose of his own cocktail mixes, the *pièce de resistance* being a 'Gin Sandwich' which comprised gin, orange juice and martini — in layers — with a dash of boysenberries!

The reasonable weather continued for another couple of days until April 29 when it started to deteriorate again. The following night we hove to under trisail with a heavy southerly swell and a high sea on top of it. We had had more than our fair share of gales since *Lion* was launched and I was beginning to wonder whether this was an omen of what was to come in the Whitbread race.

It was Sarah-Jane's birthday on May 2, but conditions were so miserable we postponed celebrating it, hoping May 3 would be a little less bumpy. It was, and SJB had the somewhat unusual distinction of completing the second year of her young but eventful life in the company of 11 adults, halfway from Auckland to Easter Island. Pippa and I were in the galley for the day, and the party went off with some style. Everyone wore paper hats, there were balloons all around the boat, and we sat down to various delights such as gourmet jelly beans, hundreds-and-thousands on bread, and muddy tea (a concoction by the Major for adults only).

Sarah-Jane, seated in her car safety seat which was lashed in position at the table aft, was quite overcome and shy for the first time ever as she opened her presents. The Doc had composed a poem for the occasion. It went:

'Playdough and swings are so much fun,
When you are a lass of only one,
But now the day for birthday two,
Has come while sailing seas of blue.
You like all the boys we can tell,
You know all their names so very well.
And to their bunks you go one by one.
What will you be like in years to come?
Your favourite birds are albatross
Who like the nappies that we toss.
We can't tell if they're colourblind.
Brown or white, do they really mind?
This sailing lark is just old hat,
And halfway around the world at that.
To you a trisail's nothing new,
Just another day of being hove to.
So happy birthday sweet SJ,
This really is a special day.
To have your second birthday at sea,
God knows what you'll be doing
By the time you're three!

Now working our way to the north-east, we were getting quite close to Easter Island. The Major, ever the entrepreneur, set up an extremely complicated sweepstake on our arrival time. He seemed to be the only one who knew how it worked, which didn't matter because he won anyway. With the temperatures climbing, the heavy clothing, which had been so necessary leaving Auckland and for the long leg east towards South America, had been packed away, for the duration, we hoped. Attire of the day was now shorts and T-shirts. SJB had her third bath of the trip, plus a haircut while Mike, a sailmaker by profession (after doing zoology at university), sewed back the leg of Harriet, SJB's favourite rag doll.

On the final day before our Easter Island landfall, the wind switched to the north and began to freshen. By the time we sighted land on May 8, with 33 miles to go, a full gale was blowing with heavy, driving rain squalls. At 1330 hours we sailed past the forbidding cliffs on the south end of the island with strong squalls roaring down the gullies and around the headlands. In one of the lulls we dropped and stowed the sails and motored to the 'anchorage' in the Vinapu roadstead, having covered the 3800 miles from Auckland in 21 days.

Rada Vinapu is a rocky indentation which would hardly qualify as a bay. It is sheltered from strong north-westerlies, but is completely exposed to the heavy swells from the Southern Ocean. This ground swell at times reached in excess of 16 feet in height and persisted for our entire stay. The pilot book information was that no north-westerly gales had been recorded at Easter Island, but it blew gale-force from that direction for two days solid. The only signs of civilisation were the six large, white oil-storage tanks which we sighted halfway up the cliffs. These serviced the 'international' airport, the runway of which ran the entire width of the island.

Andrew Troupe was to leave us here and return to New Zealand by way of Tahiti on the weekly Lan Chile flight from Santiago. We thought the flight had gone through the day before, but as we motored into Rada Vinapu, thinking there was no need to hurry, the roar of jet turbines announced that the Lan Chile jumbo was just coming in. There was not enough time for Andrew to get ashore, clear customs and make it to the airport in time to catch the flight as it left again, so he would have to stay here for a week.

A boat with two local fishermen soon arrived alongside and, with the Major fluent in Spanish, we were soon on our way to find local Chilean authorities to clear *Lion* so that we could go ashore. The rest of the crew used the time to tidy ship, inflate the Zodiac rubber dinghy and give the 30hp Evinrude a test run.

Sarah-Jane was very excited at seeing land again but had to wait before she could go ashore. She filled in time by running up and down the passageways below, which were now completely clear after the arrival clean-up. That night, with the anchorage so exposed, we kept a two-man anchor watch roster. With *Lion* only a short distance away from where the huge Southern Ocean swell was piling up in the shallower water to form into a roaring surf, it wasn't good on the nerves.

The next morning the rain had eased to showers but the wind was still gale-force, blowing unabated. Half the crew piled into the Zodiac, all wearing lifejackets and clutching the large, plastic diesel drums that needed filling when we found supplies. The rudimentary landing-place in the bay consisted of a narrow, concrete platform set in the rocky foreshore. It was only slightly protected from the incoming breakers so we had to nose the dinghy into the steps and hold it there just long enough for one person to scramble ashore with the painter. That person would keep the dinghy off the rocks while we held it back with motor going astern. We would then have to judge our moment in a lull and take the dinghy in for another two or three people to leap off onto the landing platform before repeating the process. Only half of the crew went ashore at a time, the remainder staying with the yacht in case the wind changed to the south or south-east. If that happened they would quickly have to up anchor and stand clear. It could mean that the shore party would be left to their own devices for a couple of days. There was no alternative in the circumstances.

The 'town' was on the other side of the island but only a short ride away by jeep. There we bought souvenirs and sampled the local beer while SJB sat on a horse outside the hostelry and enjoyed a cold Coke. Most of us had read Thor Heyerdahl's account of Easter Island, one of the most remote islands in the world. Heyerdahl's book *Aku Aku* had wetted our appetite for the unusual sights to be seen and our anticipation was enhanced by the fact that we had sailed from New Zealand to reach this spot. To have come in by jet aircraft would have been too easy. When the rain finally eased and the sun shone through, we went ashore again and organised a Volkswagen minibus to take us on a guided tour. The island appeared quite bleak and barren to begin with, but as we progressed, the Major's Spanish making it a lot easier to glean the niceties from our guide, I decided that it was one of the most interesting places I'd visited. Pippa described the terrain as a mixture of Dartmoor, in Devon, and Mt Wellington, in Auckland — the whole place strewn with rocks. We passed a number of temple sites as the 'road' followed the jagged black rocks of the coastline. At the eastern end of the island we turned inland and headed for a distinctive set of high, rocky outcrops. On the cliffs of these we examined one of the many quarries in which the now extinct local population had carved the massive stone statues for which Easter Island has become an anthropological curiosity. These statues, some of them weighing as much as 20 tons and standing 40 feet high, were fashioned with primitive tools and then transported many miles over rough terrain to be erected near the coastline, overlooking the sea. The 'heads' made a lasting impression on us all as we marvelled at the ingenuity of ancient man.

Next we went to the huge volcanic crater at the high, south end of the island, the road winding up to the summit through groves of wild guava. This crater alone was worth the journey from New Zealand, a most magnificent sight. We sat and looked in awe across its 1.9-kilometre bowl from the vantage point of some stone dwellings that dated back to the sixteenth or seventeenth century. Both shore parties were agog with all that they had seen when we gathered back aboard that night.

Andrew had taken his leave of *Lion* and was settled into the island's only hotel while he waited for the next Lan Chile flight to Tahiti. He was remembered as a good, if somewhat eccentric, shipmate who had arrived on board in Auckland with a kit that was complete with sextant and full log tables, Ugg boots, a set of tools, a garlic press with supply of cloves, an electric blender and an electric crêpe-maker.

That Friday night, as we motored clear in beautifully starlit conditions, we all agreed that Easter Island had been very much worth the effort. But now it was on to the Panama Canal by way of the Galapagos Islands, some 2000 miles to the north-east. The Major had managed to buy what looked an interesting assortment of fresh vegetables just before we left. He was the last person back aboard at dusk, in a heavy mist. It was quite a task to get all the produce off the landing platform and into the Zodiac by the light of torches but we accomplished it and, on the following morn, set about sorting the windfall of fresh food.

We'd stowed the haul to one side of the cockpit overnight so as not to bring any wildlife down below. We feared an infestation of cockroaches, but unearthed only a couple of small ones that appeared from time to time later on but which weren't a problem.

Lion crashed and banged her way to the north-east in easterly tradewinds under

Plenty of bird and sea life on and around the Galapagos Islands.

blue skies and bright sunshine. With some fresh 'greens' to vary the diet, life was pretty good as we again settled down to the routine of a long trip. The flying fish were appearing in great, silvery squadrons as our passage disturbed them and a number of small squid found their way onto *Lion*'s deck to provide even greater dietary variety. I cooked them to accompany drinks that evening — Calamari à la Pierre, far out into the Pacific.

By Sunday, May 19 we were 300 miles from the Galapagos Islands and only a few miles further away from the equator. We had our first real tropical weather and as the sea calmed down and the temperatures climbed, Sarah-Jane kept cool by playing in her cockpit bathtub. Like the rest of us, she was beginning to acquire a nice, deep tan. The crew had been marvellous, taking time out to keep her amused. She had reciprocated with extremely good behaviour and quite acceptable social habits — like sleeping through every night, no matter what the weather, and taking a two-hour nap at midday. The potty training had been only moderately successful thus far but SJB displayed an incredible memory for other things. She missed very much her Fru-Jus, the New Zealand-style iced juice bar on a stick.

Two days later we noticed a marked increase in marine life. The sea temperatures were quite cool because of the influence of the Humboldt Current flowing strongly up the coast of South America. But nobody fancied a swim anyhow. We had seen plenty of sharks, as well as bottle-nosed dolphins and seals. The dolphins were jumping high out of the water around the bow, so close at times that they splashed the crew who were trying to get pictures of the action. Soon after breakfast we sighted the first island in the Galapagos group — Isla Española which is the most south-eastern in the chain. Anchored close to the shore was a large Russian survey vessel.

We motored and sailed in light breezes until shortly after 1400 hours, when we dropped the pick in the anchorage of Bahia Wreck on Isla Cristobal. The captain of the port came on board and was happy to provide us with a 72-hour permit to visit. The Major and I went ashore with him to deal with immigration requirements. The Ecuadorean authorities made a point of keeping all of our passports.

The town of San Cristobal was bigger than we had expected, made up of quaint, coloured wooden houses and dusty streets. The atmosphere was pleasantly lazy and the local people very friendly. We found most of the stores we needed — diesel, fresh fruit and vegetables, and a very good local beer — then happily paid over the $30 each that allowed us, the following day, to go off in the Zodiac to see the fauna and flora for which the group is famous.

The Galapagos, or the Archipelago de Colon to give them their correct name, belong to Ecuador and have been declared an ecological zone. Special permission is needed to stay more than three days, but even so, and contrary to popular belief, the officials seem to welcome visiting yachtsmen provided they behave themselves. Tourism is becoming the main source of income. When Charles Darwin first visited these islands in HMS *Beagle,* he regarded them as a living microcosm supporting his theory of evolution. To their credit, the Ecuadoreans have done their best to preserve what Darwin saw as unique in this group.

That night, while the rest of the crew went ashore to dine at a little 'restaurant' on the beach, Pippa and I stayed aboard with Sarah-Jane. Bob came back in the dinghy to bring us dinner, the specialty of the house at the Brisas del Mar, where the rest of the team were now nicely settled in to an evening 'on the town'. It was exactly the same meal that Bob had made on board the night before, but nowhere near as good. The decibel-level increase as the evening wore on meant the crew were doing more than eating at the Brisas del Mar where the restaurant owner's 17-year-old daughter took a real shine to Bob and pronounced him the 'prettiest man in the crew'.

The next day Pippa, SJB, Alan, Dick, Tom, Fraser and I set off in the Zodiac for the short journey a few miles along the coast to Lobos Island. The sea was crystal clear, the rocks of the coastline crawling with bright, red and orange crabs. Frigate birds nestled in the dry, scrubby trees on the shoreline, the males readily identified by their bright red, inflated crops which were similar to red balloons attached to their throats. The sea-lions were extremely friendly, playing around under the Zodiac and then coming right up to us as we walked along the beaches. On Lobos, the crabs formed an orange carpet — there were so many of them — and we began to spot numbers of black marine iguanas soaking up the warmth of the sun on the rocks to the seaward side of the island. They looked like miniature dragons but could move very quickly if disturbed.

In the afternoon we swapped with the other half of the crew — Mike, the Major, Bob, Cole, Jaapi and Ginny — who had been off touring in a couple of Landrovers. It was their turn to go to Lobos while we went to the top of the island and to a seal colony not far from the town. By nightfall we were worn out and had just enough energy to pay the authorities for the diesel and collect our passports before getting under way. The stop had been all too brief. I determined that next time I passed this way I would spend longer exploring this wonderland of nature.

Panama was 700 miles away to the east and our next destination. But first we had to cross the equator. Pippa noted in her log that it was cold for the tropics — two jackets and long trousers — as we prepared for the 'crossing the line' ceremonies.

King Neptune and Queen Codfish with SJB, crossing the equator northbound.

The morning was spent making beard and crown for King and Queen Neptune, not to mention those glutinous, brown mixtures with which the initiates to Neptune's kingdom would be daubed.

Right on schedule, at 1500 hours, the good King (myself) and his sexy-looking wife Codfish (Pippa) made their appearance, much to the delight of Sarah-Jane but causing some apprehension among the 'prisoners' (those who had not crossed the equator before). These were Alan, Cole, the Doc and, of course, SJB. The first three were lashed to the shrouds where they could contemplate their fate while we dealt with the youngest member of the party. SJB's charge sheet read: 'Being heard as well as seen; failing to learn her nursery rhymes properly; and peeing on the staysail.' She was smothered in shaving foam and made to perform 'Knees Up Mother Brown' to ukelele accompaniment.

The others received somewhat harsher treatment. Dragged forth one at a time, they were first made to kiss the foot of Queen Codfish, which just happened to be plastered with mustard. They then were subjected to the customary ducking, shaving and haircutting before being forced to drink from a bottle labelled 'transvestite potion', the contents of which defied description. Alan was singled out for anointment with the 'deadly diaper'. It looked all too real but in fact was covered in a mixture of peanut butter and brown sauce.

We duly closed on Panama, celebrating Dick's elevation to grandfather status and noting the dramatic increase in shipping movements with the coast of Costa Rica just 30 miles away to port. On the last evening out, we organised a great farewell party. Alan, Dick and Tom would be getting off here. The speeches were tinged with sadness but the toasts were ardently consumed. The Doc had written another 'ode' for the occasion. To the tune of 'Jamaica Farewell', it was entitled 'Pacific Farewell' and went:

> Down de way where the boys aren't gay,
> Tom, Dick and Alan went sailing
> Dey took a trip on de Lion ship
> And when they reached Panama dey were wailing.
>
> But we're sad to say, dey going away
> Dey been with us for 43 day
> But I know that you will all agree
> Tom, Dick and Alan make a funny three.

The many verses extolled the various 'virtues' of our departing guests. One on Dick went:

> Now Dick he like the swampy air
> Especially in his bunk down dere
> And in the galley he's a whizz
> He do so many things with dem cabbages.

Of Alan:

> At night on watch he like to chat
> Of many things, dis and dat
> He knows the sea like his little town
> And he finds rogue waves so we might drown.

And of ship's captain Tom:

> Dat Partridge bloke, he's not the feathered sort
> He's an old salt from de Shipping Corp
> But he hogs da wheel like it's going to be
> De last time he'll ever put to sea.

We dropped anchor off the Balboa Yacht Club just before noon on May 27, 43 days from Auckland having covered some 6782 nautical miles. The New Zealand Line's agents in Panama, Pacific Ford, had everything laid on for us and had made all the arrangements for the canal transit. Tom Clark's son, Geoff, one of *Lion*'s sponsors through his Construction Machinery company, would be joining us for the next stage along with two of his friends, Jim Woods and Graham Shaw. Colin Kerr, B.P.'s representative, turned up to make sure we had everything we needed and to also join us for the run through to Bermuda.

At the crack of dawn the next day we joined the procession of ships bound through the canal. It was extremely hot and humid, but a more fascinating day would be hard to imagine. We lifted up through the successive locks on the Pacific side and then motored through the Gatum Lakes, surrounded by dense, tropical rain forests. Then we were lowered through the locks on the Atlantic side.

Tom, Dick and Alan were taken off by launch as soon as we anchored off Cristobal. Our friends of the last six and a half weeks were suddenly gone and another chapter in the *Lion* story was closed. We had dinner ashore with some of the 'new' crew that night, retiring early for a good sleep before setting out for Nassau, in the Bahamas, the following morning.

We reached across the Caribbean for the next three days, staying well clear of the reefs and shoals (and pirates) of the notorious Mosquito Coast. The newcomers on board settled quickly into the routine of things and warm, pink gins at 1100 hours became the norm. Geoff was also often seen in the aft cockpit with a number of cans of beer wrapped in a wet towel, trying to keep them cool. As we sailed past the western end of Cuba, making sure to keep well outside the territorial limits, the wind died, so we stopped for a swim. It was the first of many as the temperatures climbed to new heights and the sea warmed to 28 degrees Celsius.

With the wind patchy, we motor-sailed through the Florida Straits, past Great Isaacs Light and Stirrup Cay. The main diesel got a thorough workout even though the electric pump for transferring fuel from the main tanks, down in the alloy space frame, to the daily header tank had failed. We had to resort to using a modified brass bilge pump for the job, 100 strokes every hour to keep up with consumption.

By 0400 hours on June 5 we were off Nassau. We waited until 8.30 am before motor-sailing into port in company with two cruise ships. The last time Pippa and I were here was in 1978 when I was running Bob Bell's *Condor of Bermuda*. It was good to be back, and the presence on the dock of our good friend Peter Cornes only served to enhance that feeling. Peter would be joining us for the leg to Bermuda. The women didn't waste any time getting to his hotel for a bubble bath while we tidied ship and organised lunch at the Poop Deck restaurant which was renowned for Planter's Punch as well as its food. Sadly, soon after our arrival, Graham learned of the death of his father and had to dash away to catch the first flight back to New Zealand.

The crew, all fit and well and enjoying themselves immensely, had a wonderful time in Nassau even though they came off second-best to the one-armed bandits at the Paradise Island casino. Sarah-Jane just loved the beaches. She was delighted to have her feet back on dry land again.

But it wasn't all beer and skittles. There is always plenty to do on a yacht to keep things running smoothly. The *Lion* crew of Mike, Jaapi, Bob, the Doc and Cole, along with Ginny and Pippa, were totally organised with the work-lists, so getting jobs done was never a problem. Mike was proving invaluable with an amazing range of abilities. I couldn't think of anyone I would rather go to sea with or have to depend on. He was going to prove a big plus in the Whitbread race and I was privately congratulating myself on having promoted him to watch leader, when Ross Guiniven left the boat after the Sydney-Hobart race and New Zealand tour.

The wind was very light for the first day of the next stage of our journey to Bermuda, but with the water a bright blue, the sailing was most enjoyable. We stopped for our first swim in the Atlantic when the wind died completely the following day. There was a lot of sargasso weed about, but that didn't deter Sarah-Jane. She couldn't wait to jump in and made a real fuss when it was time to get her back on board so that we could continue our passage.

A few days later at 2000 hours we were motoring down the narrow channel on the northern side of Bermuda, in among the reefs, in a freshening westerly. It was inky black and visibility was poor in the occasional showers, so it was a relief to finally drop anchor at Hamilton. Our stay there would be three days in which we would ready the boat for the final part of the delivery, across the Atlantic to Cork in southern Ireland.

Peter Cornes had a house in Bermuda, so next day we moved *Lion* to a berth at the Royal Bermuda Yacht Club and Pippa, Sarah-Jane and I shifted out to spend one night in a real bed at Peter's place before the Atlantic crossing. It was a pleasant stop in a beautiful part of the world, in the company of fine people, but by now my thoughts were not of the delivery, which was almost completed anyway. My attentions were focussing increasingly on the Whitbread race and I was eager to get to Britain to prepare for the real purpose of this whole exercise.

On June 15 we bade farewell to Peter Cornes, and to Geoff Clark, Jim Woods, Colin Kerr and another guest, Vic Brown, and motored out of the channel from Bermuda. We had nobody on board except the crew and the Major for this final leg. *Lion* seemed quite empty. The 'Pond', as European yachties refer to the Atlantic, produced its share of fresh winds and one electrical storm in which *Lion* scooted along at 13 knots under triple-reefed mainsail only, with forked lightning flashing into the sea all around, accompanied by deafening thunder and torrential rain. With our mast the only tall point sticking up for miles, we felt quite vulnerable and spent an uncomfortable time banging and crashing around until, at first light, we got more sail on and pushed ahead towards our destination.

Sarah-Jane slept through it all, as was her wont every night. At daybreak, when all we wanted to do was crawl into a warm bunk, she was in top form and wanting to play games. But if our little daughter tended to be hyperactive at times, she was never sick, nor did she get too frustrated or downhearted with her unusual environment. I was sure that the experience, although unconventional, would stand her in good stead in the years ahead.

The closer we got to Ireland, the more fog we encountered so that the days rolled one into another in a grey, dank procession. The last stages of the trip were completed in a real pea-souper with our automatic, and loud, foghorn blaring away monotonously. When it was clear though, which it usually was at night, we identified an extraordinary number of satellites, so many in fact that the watches started a competition as to who had seen the most. On some of these clear nights the phosphorescence was spectacular and the inevitable dolphins looked like torpedoes as they streaked towards *Lion* trailing sparkling wakes.

Sarah-Jane was now nearly 100 percent potty-trained and we were no longer leaving a trail of disposable nappies — biodegradable of course — to mark our route. The only disadvantage to this state of affairs was that the crew was regularly called on to examine the contents of the potty and to remark on SJB's latest achievement.

We were all very sad when we heard of the loss of the Air India Jumbo jet which had gone down in the waters through which we were now sailing. The search for wreckage was still going on, based at Cork, when we at last sighted the emerald green hills of Ireland on the afternoon of Saturday, June 29. We had passed several search and salvage vessels during our last night at sea.

At 2300 hours we edged quietly into the river at Crosshaven to drop anchor within sight of the Ron Holland design office which is located in what must be one of the most charming spots in the world. We would spend three days with Ron and his team, enjoying real Irish hospitality, before moving on to the Solent where *Lion* would be based until the start of the Whitbread. The highlight of this brief pause was a Kiwi function at the Royal Cork Yacht Club, the oldest such establishment in the world, put on by the New Zealand High Commission in London in conjunction with our main sponsor Lion Breweries and the Ron Holland office. There we were, 12,000 miles from home, drinking Steinlager greens and New Zealand wine, and sampling New Zealand cheeses, in company which was an intriguing mix of Irish and Kiwi. It was as good a way as any to celebrate our arrival, even though we still had two days to go, across the Irish Sea and up the English Channel to the Solent, before the journey was completely done.

I watched Sarah-Jane mixing readily with the guests at the Royal Cork Yacht Club. She hadn't long turned two years of age, yet she had already been to places most people could only dream about. Pippa and I had worried about how she would cope with the trip, and how she would fit into an adult scene in relatively cramped surroundings. We needn't have bothered. Sarah-Jane had adapted with remarkable ease and in some ways had made the journey the more memorable for all of us. To see the delight on her face with every new experience was enchanting. With the patience and indulgence of the crew, she had developed much more quickly than a child of equal years ashore would have done. And she had an amazing recall of where she had been and what she had done — remembering clearly the statues at Easter Island, the seals at the Galapagos, swimming in the Gatum Lakes in the Panama Canal, and taking her first bubble bath at Peter Cornes' house in Bermuda. I certainly would not have wanted to do the trip without Sarah-Jane and clearly the experience had done much for her.

Potty training for Sarah-Jane.

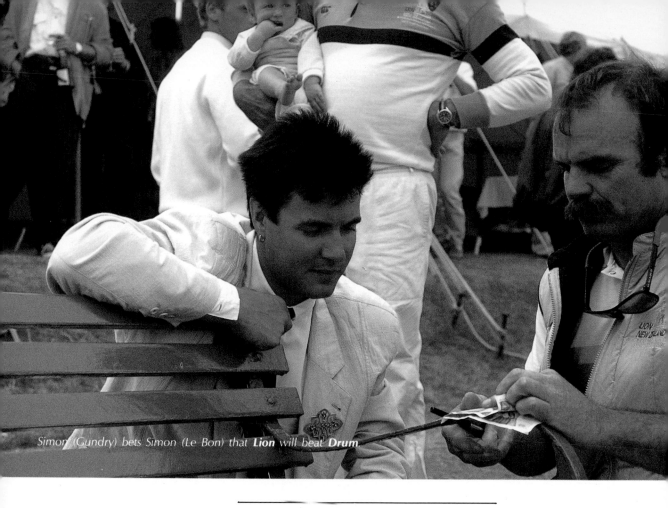
*Simon (Gundry) bets Simon (Le Bon) that **Lion** will beat **Drum.***

The time has come, the Walrus said,
to talk of many things:
of shoes — and ships — and sealing wax —
of cabbages and kings.

Lewis Carroll
The Walrus and The Carpenter

5. The Countdown Begins

Turning into the Hamble River, at the mouth of Southampton Water, to complete
the delivery journey, was a bit like coming home for those of us who had campaigned
Ceramco. This had been our base for the final build-up to the 1981-82 Whitbread,
and in the five or six weeks we had spent there we had become accepted as 'locals'
by the tight-knit community. The *Ceramco* crew had distinguished itself at the Hamble
carnival in 1981, with John Newton and Richard Macalister claiming a *Guinness Book
of Records* mark for egg-throwing and a Simon Gundry-led team winning the
wheelbarrow race which involved shoving carts up the village high street and downing
pints in four selected pubs on the route.

This time around, the *Lion New Zealand* crew formed itself into a choir to help
raise funds for the restoration of Hamble's tenth-century Norman church. In a packed
village hall, their renditions of international classics such as the 'Chesdale Cheese'

advertisement and 'Give 'em a taste of Lion' would not have been judged a threat to the Treorchy Male Voice Choir, but they brought the house down nonetheless. It was probably a good job they weren't performing in the old church, because they might have brought that down too.

As the days and weeks rolled by with a lot of work to be done to ensure *Lion* was ready for the Whitbread, the close living in Hamble's friendly atmosphere helped forge 21 men of differing ages, backgrounds and occupations into a formidable unit. There were definite characters and born leaders within the group, but the group became all. They enjoyed one another so much, and the repartee became so automatic that they became an exclusive club. But they were always friendly and generous, and those who enjoyed associate membership of that club — Hambleites such as George, the manager of the local branch of Lloyds Bank, the staff of the King and Queen Hotel, which was adopted and renamed Him and Her, and old Lenny the boatman — would not hear a bad word said about them.

There were the odd problems, of course, the sort which are inevitable when you transplant such a group of fit, eligible young males into any small community. The local young men, for example, took exception to the fact that their regular girlfriends all of a sudden became preoccupied with that carefree bunch of Kiwis who lived in the 'Pink House' on the Hamble waterfront. Some of the King and Queen regulars weren't too keen on their local being turned into a rowdy facsimile of those bars they'd seen in films from downunder. But the inherent good humour of the *Lion* guys always took the sting out of any situation that might have developed into something more serious.

Top priority when *Lion* reached the Hamble was to replace her keel with a new one which had been fabricated by Souters, in Cowes, while the boat was on its way to England, and then filled and painted by Andy Taylor, Roy Mason and Wayne Hurst so that it was ready to be fitted as soon as *Lion* was hauled out at the Moody yard and the original keel removed. Hurst, one of Auckland's leading marine paint applicators, was flown in by Epiglass to ensure that *Lion*'s underwater finish was as good as new when the job was done.

We'd decided on changing the keel after the Hobart and the run back across the Tasman to New Zealand. The Holland office, concerned with stability, had put an extra two tons of lead into the bottom of the keel just before the original one went on the boat. Apart from the implications this had in rating terms, we felt the boat was heavy and had bow-down tendencies. The new keel was a more refined shape and 1.5 tons lighter. In addition, the lead was relocated in the bottom of the keel to retain the same stability that we'd had with the original keel, while also trimming a little more by the stern. The result was a lighter boat, better trim and the same stiffness.

With the boat back in the water, we used the Seahorse maxi series on the Solent for tuning purposes. This gave us a first look at some of the opposition we would encounter in the Whitbread which was now less than two months away. The Seahorse line-up included the Farr maxis *Atlantic Privateer* and *UBS Switzerland*, *Lion*'s near sister-ship, *Drum England*, and the circuit maxi *Condor*. Also there were the Peterson 55-footer *Equity and Law*, from Holland, another Dutch entry for the Whitbread, *Philips Innovator*, a 63-footer designed by Ralph Vrolijk of Judel/Vrolijk and German Admiral's Cup team fame, and the revamped Briand 57-footer *L'Esprit D'Equipe*, skippered by France's Lionel Pean. The Seahorse series would precede the 1985-86 Admiral's Cup series and the world-famous Cowes Week regatta in which we would also encounter the Pedrick 83-footer *Nirvana,* another major force on the maxi circuit.

Lion achieved mixed results. She won one light airs race easily but in the fresher stuff, which was to predominate during the three weeks of racing that culminated in a gale-swept Fastnet classic, we began to fear that she lacked the legs against the Farr boats downwind.

The two long races in the build-up, the 200-mile Channel race and the 605-mile Fastnet, were inconclusive as far as we were concerned. In the Channel race we dragged an open propeller all the way to France on the opening leg of the course and suffered a major drop in boatspeed before we identified and corrected the fault. In the Fastnet race, we split our Kevlar mainsail in heavy upwind conditions when off Falmouth, less than a day into the race. The repair would have been a major job on board, so we withdrew in order to get the work done properly ashore and get on with what we were in England for — to ready the boat for the Round the World race.

In hindsight, the whole exercise was a waste of time, including the Seahorse series. The racing did not pertain to what we would be doing in the Whitbread and the short tacking in strong conditions only cut deeply into the life of our Kevlar racing sails. The continuous flapping in tacks, to which sails are subjected in around-the-buoys or medium-distance racing, breaks down the Kevlar cloth and drastically shortens its life-expectancy. Also, when racing around the buoys you are always striving for pointing ability, especially in a place like the Solent where you need to sail as high as possible in order to get your bow and keel the right side of a tidal flow. When open-sea racing you are rarely that hard on. You crack off a touch for boatspeed because the distances you need to cover are much greater and the weather conditions are always changing.

The concentrated racing programme did, however, prove two things. The Farr boats were quick, on all points of sailing, and would provide extremely tough opposition if they held together. The masthead-rig *Atlantic Privateer,* owned and skippered by South African-born, but United States resident, Padda Kuttel, chased *Nirvana* all the way around the Fastnet course to finish only 31 seconds astern after 605 miles. *UBS Switzerland,* skippered by Pierre Fehlmann, with a crew of dinghy sailors under his command, pulled out of the Fastnet, also with mainsail problems. But she'd shown some devastating reaching speed in the lead-up races. Both Kuttel and Fehlmann were Whitbread veterans and would know what they were doing when they got out into less confined waters.

The other point made was that the new breed of Whitbread boats would be crewed every bit as efficiently as the circuit maxis. The close-quarters jousting in the Seahorse series, mostly in 20 knots plus, produced crew work, across the fleet, that was as good as anything yet seen in maxi boats, and the standards attained on *Lion* were amongst the highest.

The Fastnet race sent a shiver down the spine of the Royal Naval Sailing Association, which organises the Whitbread, and sounded alarm bells throughout the sport as a whole. On the second day out from the Cowes start, while beating close in to the English Channel coast near Falmouth, the keel fell off *Drum England* and she capsized. A terrible tragedy was avoided only because *Drum* couldn't have picked a better time or place to perform what could have been a death roll. She was in full view of the shore, just a couple of miles off, and being watched by two coastguard observers taking their lunch-break when she went bottom up. They raised the alarm immediately and within 10 minutes a helicopter from nearby Culdrose air-sea-rescue

Drum England

base was hovering overhead and winching down a survival expert.

As *Drum* rolled, with almost slow deliberation, two of her crew — one of them designer Ron Holland's brother, Phil — had the survival instinct to walk around the hull and take up secure positions near the rudder. From there they were able to haul their crewmates up the impossibly smooth underwater sections of the upturned maxi using the straps of two lifejackets as a lifeline. Most of *Drum*'s crew had been thrown into the water when they couldn't find a grip on the slippery topsides. They made it back to the boat and found some security by standing on the top (now bottom) guardrail and gripping the boat's toerail. Even so, they had to snatch deep breaths and hang on for dear life as *Drum* wallowed in the swells.

The 16 people in the water were soon hauled to what was only the relative safety of the upturned hull where they were now subjected to the problem of hypothermia. Six others, including pop star Simon Le Bon, were still inside the boat, one of them trapped in his bunk and in danger of drowning as the water-level rose until *Drum* stabilised. These six were brought to the surface by the chopper's diver and the operation of winching everyone to safety began, the coldest first. The chopper made quick dashes to the nearby shore to unload and return for more. By the time this operation began, several of the half-clad people who had been offwatch below when the boat rolled were very cold and shivering violently. If help hadn't been so close to hand — everyone was ashore within half an hour of *Drum*'s rolling — who knows what the outcome would have been.

What, people asked, would have been the result if *Drum* had turned turtle out in the middle of the ocean in the Whitbread, or even if it had happened where it did, but at night and unobserved? The inquiries began immediately as Le Bon and his business partners, Paul and Mike Berrow, organised salvage of their stricken maxi and assessed whether they could effect a second resurrection of the boat in time for the Whitbread start on September 28. The task was daunting. *Drum* had rolled on August 11. Her keel was lost in 60 feet of water, her mast was wrecked, her sails were in ruins and there was damage to her deck. Le Bon and the Berrows had less than seven weeks in which to achieve what appeared a small miracle, even if they could get their hands on *Drum* which had been claimed as a salvage prize by Cornish fishermen.

Drum's keel had snapped off at the hull when welds in the upper keel frame structure failed. Ballast is only one function of a yacht's keel which also is a wing-like shape beneath the yacht to provide the lift to enable that yacht to sail close to the wind. To achieve the right shapes, most maxi keels are fabricated in aluminium. The required amount of lead ballast is securely moulded into the lower part of the aluminium boxwork. The finished product is welded to an aluminium gridwork built into the floor of the yacht and through-bolted into the internal framing. It was a system which, in Holland's case, had been proven in *Kialoa* and *Condor* and, so far, in *Lion*. With *Drum,* however, it seemed that the work had not been done to specifications. The keel had flexed from side to side and finally snapped off, leaving the keel bolts still in the hull. The Woolfson Unit at Southampton University, in an independent investigation into the mishap, found that the all-important welds were porous and had insufficient penetration, or none at all.

Because *Lion's* keel was similarly engineered, the question was whether she too might be suspect. The answer most emphatically was 'no'. The work on both her keels had been faithfully carried out, the welds inspected and X-rayed. She had come through the toughest Sydney-Hobart race on record, experienced 70-knot winds on the New Zealand coast during her national fundraising tour, and reached Britain on her own bottom with not even a hint of movement by her original keel. The replacement was built and fitted to the same specifications with the same careful checking of the work. It had been through a copious amount of rough weather in the Seahorse series, the Channel race and the Fastnet, and again there was not even a sign of problems. I was completely satisfied that *Lion's* appendage would last the distance.

By the time the smoke of all this cleared, the Whitbread fleet had been confirmed at 15 boats — if Le Bon and the Berrows, with Skip Novak fronting the operation, could bring *Drum* back from the dead. At first glance, that total was not impressive when you compared it with 17 starters for the first race in 1973-74, 15 in 1977-78, and 29 in 1981-82. But six of the 1985-86 fleet — seven if you included the veteran Gurney 77-footer *Norsk Data GB* — were maxis. The six newcomers to the maxi ranks were specially built for the event and would race off the stick in a special division while also competing for the overall corrected time prize.

Atlantic Privateer had to start favourite for line honours in view of her performances in the 1984 South Atlantic race (Cape Town to Punta del Este), in which she broke the record in her competitive debut, in the Seahorse series and in the Channel and Fastnet races. The Fastnet was probably the real indication of her potential. In what was predominantly a two-sail reach in mostly gale conditions, *Atlantic Privateer* finished second across the line and emerged top maxi on corrected time while fourth in the overall fleet, which included many of the most competitive and best-sailed offshore racers in the world.

Atlantic Privateer

Kuttel, who raced the 1981-82 Whitbread with his Swan 65 *Xargo III,* would have on board a strong mix of international boat-professionals, that nomadic breed of person who makes sailing his life and is in great demand to crew the racing maxis or to skipper someone's large cruising yacht. Kuttel's sailing master would be another hard-driving South African, David Bongers, who was perhaps his country's best-known sailor.

But Bongers might also prove to be Kuttel's weak link. In the final weeks before the race, when the Whitbread crews were in constant touch with one another, working on their boats at the Moody yard or mixing in the bar of the nearby Ship Inn, Bongers became increasingly insistent that *Atlantic Privateer* was the best boat in the race and would lick the opposition. He was also, on one occasion, heard to add: 'That's if I don't pull the bloody mast out of the boat.' It was a strangely prophetic aside, as we were soon to find out.

Bongers' concern about *Atlantic Privateer*'s mast was legitimate and shared by more than one astute observer. The spar was that with which *Flyer* had done the double in 1981-82 and which had been subjected to its share of hard miles. Everyone, at first, thought *Flyer*'s spar was a temporary expediency on Kuttel's part while he assessed the merits of a masthead rig as opposed to fractional. But the spar stayed, and the doubts about that spar circulated freely.

UBS Switzerland, another new Farr maxi but with a fractional rig, would have been second favourite with the punters. This would be skipper Pierre Fehlmann's third Whitbread and he had prepared immaculately, beginning his organising almost as soon as he had finished the 1981-82 race with the Farr 60-footer *Disque D'Or. UBS Switzerland* was quite a story. She had been built with great attention to weight, using the very latest fibreglass construction techniques as they applied to Kevlar, near the end of the main runway at Geneva's international airport. When hull and decks were complete, Fehlmann solved the problem of having a maxi many miles from the ocean by loading *UBS* inside a Super Guppy, one of the world's largest military transport aircraft, to fly her to Toulon on the Mediterranean.

Fehlmann's build-up with a crew of mostly dinghy sailors, some of them Olympic 470-class people, had included the 1985 SORC (Southern Ocean Racing Conference) off Florida, the Seahorse series and the Channel and Fastnet races. *UBS* was longer and lighter than the other Farr maxis in the race, with slightly less sail. The harder it blew the more potent she would be, and Fehlmann was one of the most experienced skippers in the race with two fourths on corrected time to his credit.

The third Farr maxi, another fractional, was our New Zealand rival, *NZI Enterprise*, skippered by Digby Taylor, who had won a lot of respect for his 1981-82 Whitbread campaign with *Outward Bound,* which had finished fifth on corrected time. But Taylor had started his 1985-86 run late and his project had been plagued with delays and controversy as he tried to reinvent the wheel at every turn, in construction techniques, winch systems, fittings and sails.

The public of New Zealand seemed to develop a love-hate view of the two Kiwi maxis. Taylor presented a 'poor relation, good old New Zealand country boy' image and sections of the media responded to this. The average Kiwi believed that *Lion* had all the money she needed and, with multiple corporate support, had access to a limitless cheque book, while Taylor was on the bare bones of his bum but giving it a good old Kiwi try. The result was that much of the nation seemed to love *NZI* and hate *Lion.* The *Lion* crew and myself tried our best to ignore what we knew to be an unfair situation, as we respected Taylor's boat and got on well with his crew.

There was no limitless cheque book to fund *Lion*'s campaign. We were struggling just as hard as Taylor and his support team to raise the money we would need to campaign the boat. We had the advantage of the excellent sponsorship package which Tom Clark had put together to get *Lion* in the water, but it wasn't our fault that Taylor had been second cab off the rank in this department. When the media bias was at its worst, I was sorely tempted to reply, but a public slanging match would have done neither campaign any good, so I concentrated on keeping our effort on the rails and on schedule.

One thing which confounded me was the reluctance of the New Zealand media to tell the truth about what was going on. They knew the problems Taylor was having and they were aware of unrest amongst the crew. Taylor had some very good people in his line-up — guys like Murray Ross, Mike Keeton, Ross Field and Steve Wilson, who had a lot of top ocean-racing miles to their credit. They and the rest of the crew were stretched to the limit in a programme which was well behind schedule and, inevitably, their disillusionment became public knowledge. But the media mostly, and inexplicably, ignored the facts of the situation.

While *Lion* was at a high state of readiness and racing the Seahorse series, *NZI* was in the process of a trouble-plagued delivery trip to Britain on her own bottom, a decision that was difficult to comprehend. Taylor could have shipped *NZI* on the same vessel that brought the New Zealand Admiral's Cup team boats to the northern hemisphere. His programme was a long way behind schedule and his crew, who had been flat out building the boat and trying to get it ready for departure, could have done with a break. But Taylor insisted on sailing to Britain.

ion takes Air New Zealand under Tower Bridge.

Cote D'Or

NZI's progress was unfortunately beset by problems and these culminated in her running hard aground on a dangerous reef in the Caribbean. Taylor put into Fort Lauderdale, allegedly for electrical repairs. But a badly twisted and mangled keel was revealed when NZI was hauled from the water. NZI was apparently in such dire straits at one stage on the reef that the liferafts were brought on deck and the crew's passports and items of value were stowed in those rafts ready for a speedy evacuation.

Despite these problems, the fact remained that NZI came from one of the best design offices in the world and had shown real speed on most points of sailing during her fundraising tour of New Zealand and on her U.K. delivery. With people like Murray Ross on board, she had to rank as a major contender.

The 83ft Joubert-Nivelt design *Cote D'Or,* to be skippered by the legendary French distance-racer Eric Tabarly, was an unknown quantity. Her origins were French but she was sponsored by a Belgian chocolate manufacturer, and so was entered by Belgium. The longest boat in the race, she had a masthead rig which looked a little short and she had displayed some disturbing bow-down tendencies when she spinnaker-ran through the Channel race fleet on her way to Cowes for the Fastnet classic.

But Tabarly's skill and experience had to be respected. He'd already worked wonders to get the boat to the Solent at all. Unable to find a sponsor in his native France, he'd come up with his Belgian backer desperately late in the piece and had had to persuade the Amtec yard in Willebroeck to work three shifts a day, seven days a week to complete construction in time. With no build-up whatsoever, *Cote D'Or* did remarkably well in the Fastnet, finishing third across the line — five hours behind *Nirvana* and *Atlantic Privateer* but five minutes ahead of *Condor*.

Lion's near sister-ship, *Drum*, was going to make it to the start. The Royal Naval Sailing Association offered Le Bon and the Berrows two weeks' dispensation so that they could start the race 14 days after the rest of the fleet. But they declined the offer and pressed on with replacing *Drum's* keel and rig and refurbishing her electronics and sail wardrobe. Skip Novak marshalled the best resources in southern England to do the work and kept everyone up to the almost impossibly tight schedule.

Drum's new keel was designed and engineered by the Holland office and built by Souters, of Cowes, who had done *Lion's* replacement. The new appendage was similar to that for *Lion* with a more vertical leading edge, a hint of the elliptical approach in the trailing edge, and all ballast concentrated in the bottom of the keel to allow internal ballast to be dumped. For a mast, *Drum* would use the spare for the Spanish-owned Frers maxi *Xargo*, a development of the *Flyer* rig which was now in *Atlantic Privateer*. This spar was 1100lbs lighter than the original, which had been ruined in the capsize and cut free so that the inverted *Drum* could be towed into Falmouth Harbour. The changes, in ballast and rig, meant that *Drum* would be significantly lighter than *Lion* for the race, but it remained to be seen how quickly her crew regained their confidence in a boat which had recently turned turtle under them.

For all practical purposes one had to forget about *Norsk Data GB* in the maxi stakes. Even though she was big enough to be a contender, she would be undertaking her fifth racing circumnavigation. A development of the legendary circuit maxi *Windward Passage*, she had been built by Chay Blyth for the inaugural 1973-74 Whitbread and, as *GB II*, had been first to finish in a time of 144 days 10 hours 43

Philips Innovator

NZI Enterprise

69

UBS Switzerland

minutes 44 seconds. In 1977-78, skippered this time by Rob James, she broke her own record with a time of 134 days 12 hours 22 minutes 47 seconds and again was first to finish.

In 1981-82, skippered again by Blyth but renamed *United Friendly,* she went around in 143 days 22 hours 23 minutes 50 seconds. In between times, she had taken line honours in the *Financial Times* Clipper Race, from Portsmouth to Sydney and back. Now dated in design with much of her original equipment still aboard, *Norsk Data GB* would be too tired to foot it with the young upstart maxis in the 1985-86 fleet.

Although *Lion* was a couple of feet shorter than the boat I originally had in mind — 78ft instead of 80ft overall — and rated 1.4ft under the maxi limit of 70ft, we had the utmost faith in her ability even though the Farr boats might have the legs on her in fresh downwind conditions. She was a real powerhouse to windward in all conditions and fast on all points of sail in the lighter stuff. What could be just as important, however, was that she was built to finish the Whitbread, and that wasn't necessarily true of her opposition. In the quest for lightness they had, in my view, cut corners which would prove their undoing if the 1985-86 race was anything like the previous three Whitbreads. There was already evidence of this, with frames cracking and hulls flexing even in the relatively sheltered English Channel. What would happen if the Southern Ocean really turned it on?

One of the main Whitbread handicap contenders *Philips Innovator,* a 63ft Vrolijk design in aluminium, had returned to her builders after the Fastnet race for strengthening of her hull around the keel. Dutchman Dirk Nauta had put together a carefully structured challenge with the full backing of the international giant Philips. He'd raced his boat in the 1985 SORC, returned to Holland for a new keel and a lighter, taller

L'Esprit D'Equipe

---

spar, and then showed the yacht's full potential in the Seahorse series. Nauta raced *Tielsa* in the 1977-78 Whitbread and had also done the *Financial Times* race and the Spice race from Holland to Java. He would be one to watch.

The surprise in the pack might be the 57ft Briand design *L'Esprit D'Equipe* which raced the 1981-82 Whitbread as *33 Export*. She was dismasted in leg two and had to abandon the race. Bought by the French-based computer consortium Bull, and renamed as a focus for company spirit, she was skippered by the talented and durable Lionel Pean who had proved his credentials in the highly competitive world of French offshore racing, including winning the 1983 Figaro solo Half Ton event. *L'Esprit* won every race in the Seahorse series on corrected time and with a small, hard-driving crew would make life difficult for everyone if the breaks around the world tended the small boat way.

1985-86 WHITBREAD ROUND THE WORLD RACE FLEET

Boat	Country	Owner/Skipper	Designer	LOA	Rig	Rating	Construction
Atlantic Privateer	USA	Peter Kuttel	Farr	80ft	M/Head	69.5ft	Kevlar
Norsk Data GB	U.K.	Bob Salmon	Gurney	77ft	M/Head	67.1ft	Sandwich
Cote D'Or	Belgium	Eric Tabarly	Joubert/Nivelt	83ft	M/Head	69.6ft	Kevlar
Drum England	U.K.	Skip Novak	Holland	77ft	M/Head	69.2ft	Kevlar
Equity And Law	Holland	Pleun van der Lugt	Holland	55ft	M/Head	44.3ft	GRP
Fazer Finland	Finland	Michael Berner	Frers	65ft	M/Head	53.3ft	GRP
Fortuna Lights	Spain	Javier Visiers	Visiers	63ft	M/Head	49.5ft	GRP
L'Esprit D'Equipe	France	Lionel Pean	Briand	57ft	Fractional	46.5ft	Alloy
Lion New Zealand	N.Z.	Peter Blake	Holland	78ft	M/Head	68.6ft	Kevlar
NZI Enterprise	N.Z.	Digby Taylor	Farr	80ft	Fractional	70.0ft	Kevlar
Philips Innovator	Holland	Dirk Nauta	Judel/Vrolijk	63ft	Fractional	52.2ft	Alloy
Rucanor Tristar	Belgium	Gustaaf Versluys	Dumas	58ft	Fractional	45.6ft	Kevlar
SAS Baia Viking	Denmark	Jesper Norsk	Elvstrom/ Kjaerulff	50ft	M/Head	41.4ft	Steel
Shadow of Switzerland	Switzerland	N. Zehender-Mueller	S. & S.	57ft	M/Head	41.3ft	GRP
UBS Switzerland	Switzerland	Pierre Fehlmann	Farr	80ft	Fractional	69.4ft	Kevlar

*Eve of departure at Gosport with **Lion** all snugged down and ready to go.*

For some were sunk and many were shattered, and so
could fight us no more —
God of battles, was ever a battle like this in the
world before?

Alfred, Lord Tennyson
The Revenge

6. The Moment of Truth

Saturday, September 28: Whitbread race start day. Time to remember that old yachting
adage: 'When the gun goes, the bullshit stops.'

The boat and crew were as ready as they'd ever be. In the last few days before
the start, the Camper and Nicholson marina at Gosport, where the 15-boat Round
the World race fleet was assembled, had become a scene of increasingly frantic activity.
Even on the morning of the start there were major jobs being done on a number
of yachts, including *NZI Enterprise.*

Lion, in the midst of it all, was like an oasis in a desert. We'd finished all the
pre-race checks days earlier, and locked the boat up to be away from the madding
crowd until the last-minute loading of the small amount of fresh food we would be
taking. The crew was in a similar state of preparedness. Tom Clark had given them
one of his famous 'Go get 'em boys' team-talks the day before. They loved it, but

it probably wasn't necessary. I don't think I'd ever seen a large team of competitors so tightly knit in spirit or so determined to succeed.

It was nearly 12 months since they had been named as the crew of *Lion New Zealand* and in that time we'd had only one defection. Ross Guiniven had quit after the Sydney-Hobart race and the fundraising tour of New Zealand. He'd given business concerns as his reason for doing so, which was fair enough considering the massive commitment which the project required. The fundraising tour had been structured to expose the crew to that commitment, to make everyone absolutely aware of what they were letting themselves in for.

Roscoe's departure gave me the opportunity to promote Mike Quilter to watch leader, a role which he assumed quite naturally and performed almost to perfection, and to introduce Guy Beaumont to the *Lion* complement. A big and strong Wellington yachtie, Guy had applied to join the crew at a time when my list was all but complete. I wasn't looking for any more general hands. But with a vacancy to fill, a man with a background of maxi racing on *Condor* was a logical choice. I telephoned Guy and he asked for a couple of days to assess his business commitments. When he returned my call he was all go. His introduction to the other 20 people in the line-up was hectic, at the 11th hour before the boat was due to leave for England. But he quickly found his niche in the scheme of things and was readily accepted and respected by the 'old guard'.

As we motored *Lion* out of Portsmouth Harbour and into a decidedly misty Solent

Guy Beaumont (Combo), 27, company director — fitted readily into the crew and quickly joined in the fun.

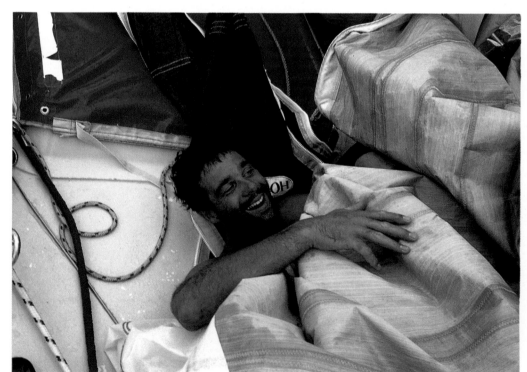

The fog closes in to make life difficult with so many spectator boats around.

to the start area off Gilkicker Point, I gathered everyone around the cockpit area for a final 'briefing'. I didn't need to tell anyone what to do or what was expected of them. They'd lived this project for more than a year now and were about to give up the best part of another year to see it through. They certainly didn't need reminding just how much was on the line, nor of the hopes and expectations of the folks back home that would be riding with them.

But I did want to put things into perspective, *Lion*'s performance included. We'd taken quite a lot of flak after the Seahorse series and the Channel and Fastnet races. *Lion* had been labelled 'too heavy' and 'off the pace'. Deep down, we all suspected that there was an element of truth in both of those jibes. *Lion* was a maxi which, in this Whitbread fleet, wasn't quite a maxi so there would be times, when length was the determining factor, that she would lack the legs against the longer Farr boats. She also was heavier than the boat that I had set out to achieve. I'd never said that publicly, but we'd weighed the boat and I knew the figures. But *Lion* had also been built and geared up to withstand the rigours of the Whitbread race. Barring something over which we had no control, she would be there at the finish, no matter what the elements and the major oceans of the world decided to deal to her. I suspected that some of our opponents would not.

I conveyed these convictions to the crew in the final minutes before we hoisted sail for the start countdown. There would be times when *Lion* would need all the help that we could give her to keep up. There would be times when we would be

*The Needles channel with **NZI Enterprise** astern as we turn right for Cape Town.*

grateful for her pedigree and her integrity. She was the strongest boat in the race with the best crew. All I could ask for was everyone's best shot. For the rest of it, nature would take its course.

The start was a shambles. The fog in the Solent was thick enough to obscure much of the mile-long start-line, but that wasn't the problem — the spectator fleet was. Milling around in the mist were hundreds of boats of all sizes and descriptions. There had been no serious pre-race campaign to educate people as to where they should and should not go during the start proceedings, so the scene was chaotic.

Race officials delayed the gun by 20 minutes while they vainly attempted to achieve some order. But finally they had to concede defeat and start regardless. In the confusion, both *Drum* and the Belgian entry *Rucanor Tristar,* a 58ft Dumas design, were in collision with spectator craft. The damage, fortunately, was not serious except to the eardrums of those on the spectator boats.

A fickle north-easterly made it a spinnaker departure with just enough puff to get us going. The fog dampened the scene somewhat but it was still a moment to remember as we went for the middle of the line with nobody anywhere near us. Now all we had to do was safely negotiate the 10 miles of the Solent, sniffing our way through the fog and dodging the traffic, to reach the sanctuary of the English Channel.

Drum got the best of it going down the Solent. They had crack helmsman and Solent expert Lawrie Smith on board for the first leg to Cape Town. He called everything right on the way to the Needles so that *Drum* was first out into the Channel by a handy margin. We had worked more towards the mainland shore early on and were on the wrong side of a shift off the entrance to Southampton Water.

By the time we reached the Needles, however, we were hard on the stern of *NZI Enterprise,* tight spinnaker reaching in eight knots of wind and flat water. She started to defend her position as we moved in to attack, sharpening up to hold on to the windward berth. But her spinnaker unclipped from the pole and she slowed dramatically. *Lion* slid through her lee and set out after *Drum* and *Atlantic Privateer,* with *UBS Switzerland* down to leeward of us. *Cote D'Or* was bringing up the rear of the maxis group, looking a bit sticky in the light airs.

The *Lion* crew were still chuckling about the preliminaries to our little dice with *NZI.* As we moved in to within 100 metres of *NZI*'s port quarter, her supporters' boat camped right in front of us and fed us its propeller wash. We waved at them for several minutes, asking them to get out of the way, but they ignored us. I blew my cool and whipped down below to grab *Lion*'s Very pistol, a mean-looking 38mm bore job. When the *NZI* supporter group saw me coming back on deck cocking the pistol and making my intentions absolutely clear, they got the message in a hurry and scooted clear. The pistol wasn't loaded, of course, but I must have been pretty convincing. The *Lion* guys thought I'd gone mad and promptly nicknamed me 'Rambo'.

The English Channel was in a docile mood as we slipped along for the rest of the afternoon, under full main, 1.5oz reacher and staysail, with a steady 12 knots of breeze just forward of the beam. *Drum* and *Atlantic Privateer* slipped in and out of the mist in the distance ahead of us. We were holding them but *NZI* eased through to windward.

By 2000 hours the breeze was a south-easterly at 15 knots and we'd changed to the 1.5oz spinnaker. *Cote D'Or* appeared out of the murk astern and slipped through our lee. Her extra length was making itself felt but she couldn't shake us once she'd

A beautiful sunset off the Canary Islands.

got her nose in front. We now had *Cote D'Or* 200 metres dead ahead and *NZI* 300 metres off our for'ard beam to windward, with *Drum* and *Atlantic Privateer* still visible a bit further in the distance. It was going to be some race if it continued in this fashion.

By this stage I had informed the race committee by radio that I was protesting about *UBS* flying spinnakers that did not comply with the race rules pertaining to what you were allowed to wear in the form of sponsor logos. *Philips Innovator* was doing it too. I'd already had a go at the committee, before the start, about the signwriting on *UBS* which was absolutely contrary to the rules, but they red-facedly told me they had amended the rules in question two weeks earlier, and *UBS* complied with the amendments. If they had done this, I certainly hadn't been informed and that too was a requirement. Now Fehlmann was using spinnakers which had all sorts of sponsor mentions that weren't allowed.

I didn't think I'd get anywhere with my complaint, but was determined to make an issue of the point. With *Lion,* we had complied strictly with all the rules, particularly with the way we had painted the names of our subsidiary sponsors around the topsides just below the gunwhale. If I'd known that the rules weren't going to be enforced, I would have given those sponsors better exposure. And if sponsors' names could be flown on *UBS* spinnakers, I could have left Air New Zealand and the New Zealand Line emblazoned all over ours. My concern was that if the race committee was going to turn a blind eye to these infringements, what would their position be when confronted with more serious breaches of the regulations. The continentals were already getting away with blue murder.

The weather continued light for the next 24 hours. We'd lost Tabarly and *Cote D'Or* when he cut the corner off Ushant by going inside Ile d'Ouessant. I was tempted to do the same as the channel is clear enough. But I was worried about adverse tide so we went the longer way around. When we got the Argos satellite plot of the fleet some hours later I was relieved to find that I had called it right. *Cote D'Or* was trapped inside Ushant with no wind while we were still in touch with the leaders *Drum* and *Atlantic Privateer,* although we couldn't see anyone in the thick fog.

Simon had been catching up on his sleep during these first couple of days of the race while it was quiet — an old hand charging the battery for harder times to come — and was doing quite a bit of napping on deck. Balls, wearing a bear-hunter's hat against the cold, reckoned sleeping Simon was his first 'kill' of the trip. This was a busy time for me, close to the French coast as we approached the Bay of Biscay, with a lot of shipping in the vicinity. But I kept track of things through the ship's log which was already spiced with literary gems such as 'Doctor's yawn a wonderful shade of green' and 'Maybe Glen has morning sickness'.

Tuesday, October 1 was my birthday and we celebrated by tacking out to sea in a 25-knot southerly, heading for a frontal system coming in from the Atlantic which I thought looked promising. There were still only about eight miles separating the maxis and this was our first opportunity to try something smart. At about 0400 hours we got the westerly change I was hoping for, and tacked back on to starboard, laying course with a nice windward advantage on our rivals.

The next few days showed that *UBS* had done the same as us but had held on to port tack longer to make an even greater gain on the fleet. The log reported: 'Ten pommy passport applications filed by Dalts' watch after brilliant tactical sailing by Low Life's boys.' 'Low Life' was the nickname given to Mike Quilter, the rest of the crew reckoning he was, with some sexual connotation, the lowest form of life on earth. The competition between the two watches was already intense and was again evidenced by the log which read: 'After superb sailing by the Black Watch (Mike's team), we've stuffed it right up *Drum* and *Atlantic Privateer* overnight. Now it's up to Dalton's spongy puds to try to keep it up.'

Noon positions on the Wednesday showed us to be level-pegging with *UBS* which was further to sea than us. *Atlantic Privateer* was 27 miles astern, while *Drum* was 56 miles back and in trouble closer in to the shore. There was no report of *NZI* which had a generator fault and was faced with the prospect of having to divert to the Canary Islands to take on spare parts. *Fazer Finland* had similar problems. *UBS* had unwittingly lost an emergency radio beacon over the side. The transmitter had begun operating as soon as the beacon hit the water, sending automatic distress calls through communications satellites. The search and rescue people got quite concerned that there was a vessel in trouble off the north-west corner of Spain, until the source of the signals was traced and identified.

While the rescue authorities were dealing with his beacon inshore, *UBS* was in fact 70 miles further to sea than *Lion* and three miles ahead of us in terms of distance to go. Both of us kept opening out on the boats astern and the added good news was that *NZI* was back there with them.

By October 3 we had *Atlantic Privateer* and *NZI* 60 miles astern, with *Drum* 25 miles behind them. *Cote D'Or* still hadn't recovered from her Ushant experience and was 120 miles back. My attentions, however, were focussed on the Canary Islands. We were two days ahead of where we were at the same time in the last race, which meant we were going 25 percent faster. But there looked to be lighter weather in the offing and in the match-racing situation we were enjoying, we'd only have to sneeze and we'd have everyone breathing down our necks again.

Life on the weather rail was illuminating. The log explained: 'Beaumont-Ford Farming Inc. annual deer sale now taking place on weather deck. A. Hansen, of Dalgety, conducting said auction which will be followed by Lion New Zealand sheep dog trials, Trae (Tony) defending his title.' This was followed the next day, Doc's birthday, by: 'The on-deck deer auction and sheep dog trials going well. Dog Blue needs training. Dalgetys gain fencing contract for deer farm. Guy Beaumont voted Young Farmer of the Year so will shout tonight at the Murupara pub.' And, after the first showers of the trip as the weather got decidedly stickier: 'Dalton's watch renamed the Pink Watch. They may be slow but they do smell ever so sweet. The Black Watch may smell bad, but they are faaast.'

The fast progress was too good to last. On October 4 we ran into our own private calm patch and waffled along at around three knots while *UBS*, further to sea, held the breeze and opened up a gap of 50 miles. The boats astern had run down on us, so that our second place in the fleet was under threat. The weather maps showed that a small high had developed overnight, right on top of us. But that was ocean racing and we began to get breeze again while the boats astern ran into our light patch. A lot of damage had been done, however. *Atlantic Privateer* had closed to within 30 miles of us and, while we were doing only 50 miles, *Cote D'Or* had done 120 miles and was now only about 60 miles astern.

I was already printing out weather maps for further south on the track — the ones from Dakar were the best at this stage — to try to dodge any more traps, and soon I would be keeping a close watch on the Doldrums in order to build up a full scenario before choosing the way we would go through.

One week into the leg we were making eight knots in a 10-knot north-north-

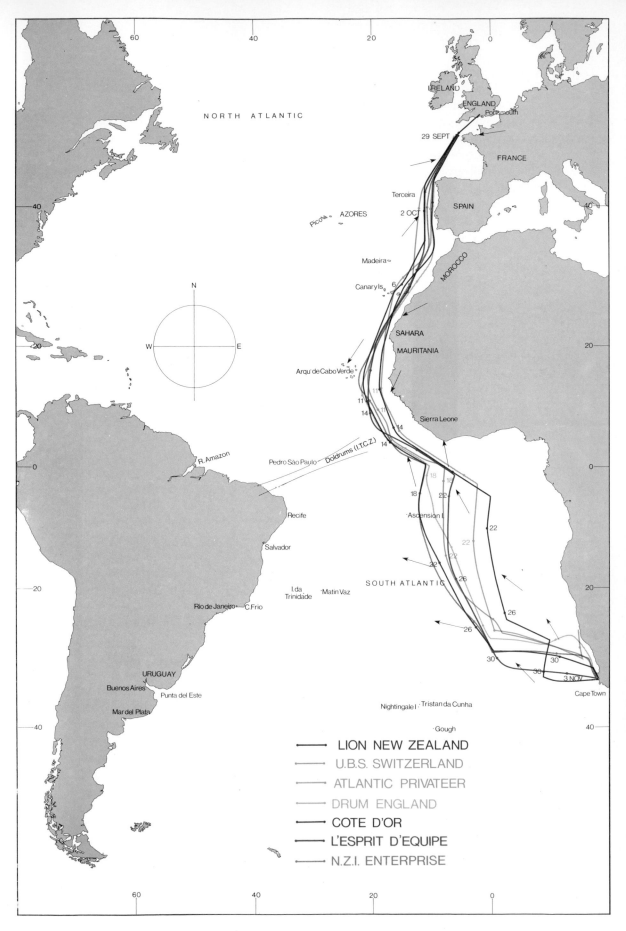

LEG 1 PORTSMOUTH-CAPE TOWN

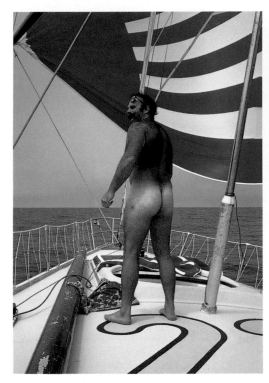

*A race 'vet', Simon had his own dress habits for the foredeck (left), and kept a detailed log for his column in **NZ Yachting** magazine.*

easterly. We were holding the boats astern but *UBS* had snuck away to a lead of 120 miles, averaging three knots more than us in a 24-hour period. *Drum,* for some reason, was right in on the coast off Casablanca, with the smaller yachts like *Philips Innovator,* which hadn't slowed at all, snapping at her heels. We'd been done by *UBS* and we didn't like it. Maybe if we'd gone 30 miles further out to sea coming down the coast of Portugal we'd have been right up with her. But . . .

UBS was reporting only 5-10 knots of wind from the north-west. We were starting to get a wriggle-on again in a northerly, so we had our fingers, and everything else, crossed. *Lion* was going well and the crew were absolutely tireless in the pursuit. Down through the Canary Islands, we picked up a 12-knot tailwind off Lanzarote which freshened to 20 knots as we shot through the gap between Gran Canaria and Fuerteventura, only about 10 miles off the shore. We charged through the night with the big 1.5oz spinnaker. But it was shortlived.

By the morning we were back to the light-air kite and shooter. Still, we made good time all day, peeling up and down the kite range as the wind increased, then decreased, *Lion* going really well. We closed 35 miles on *UBS* so that she was back to 145 miles in front of us, but we had the feeling that *NZI* was not far away from *Lion. Cote D'Or* and the boats further astern weren't having such a good time of it. While we were running at 11 knots, they were reporting light headwinds and calms. It must have been trying for Tabarly, knowing that we were 200 miles ahead of him with *UBS* another 145 miles in front of that.

The following day, October 7, we learned that we'd closed a couple of miles on *UBS* and were 50 miles ahead of *NZI*, which appeared to have had a better run than us through the Canaries. *Atlantic Privateer* was 80 miles astern so we'd done a tidy little job on her. *Drum* was beginning to recover and was 25 miles astern of *Atlantic Privateer*. But *Cote D'Or* was still more than 200 miles behind *Lion* and struggling to make any impression. I had to admit, although it was hard on the nerves, that I was beginning to like the daily position updates. It was a far cry from previous races when you had to report only twice in a seven-day period, and it had to be good for public interest ashore. *Lion* was now second on the water and second on corrected time — *UBS* leading both categories. But the Doldrums were coming up fast and we could pull her in very quickly if Fehlmann got it wrong in the windless belt.

The humour on board continued unabated. Raw Meat was proving a natural jester and the log recorded: 'R. Meat challenged reigning arm-wrestling champ Dalts and got done like a dinner. He's now training 10 hours a day on the grinders. Meanwhile, staysail up and down more often than Whale's (Aran) shorts. Jaapi teaching the boys some smooth lines in Afrikaans.' The following day's entries included: 'Combo (Guy), with an advance from his friendly BNZ manager, has opened a branch of State Insurance in the forepeak. He is now selling cigarettes at a modest fee to cover the risk aforementioned in Cape Town.' The 'aforementioned' risk was the preceding log entry which noted: 'Statement of the night, by Mr Roy Mason — Give me a cigarette and I won't hit you when I'm drunk.'

The next night the watch below couldn't sleep for laughing. With *Lion* barrelling along in 20-knot tailwinds and closing on *UBS*, the deck watch was trimming by animal noises. Two dog barks meant shooter sheet in, one bark meant shooter sheet stop. A moo signalled shooter halyard up and a baa meant spinnaker sheet in. And so it went for hours, the boat cutting a real dash while the whole crew was in hysterics.

NZI Enterprise in sight off the Cape Verde Islands.

Polar tables in the cockpit listed performance targets while the B&G gear shows 10 knots of boatspeed with 14.8 knots of wind aft of abeam.

It really was 'Old McDonald's Farm' stuff.

On we sped with Raw Meat first to claim a record burst of 15.61 knots. Simon topped that with 17.18 after the watch changed, then Combo did 'a controlled 19.11 knots' as *Lion* made 50 miles in four hours. We were 17 degrees North 20 degrees West, approximately, and by this stage in 1981-82 we were into the Doldrums. But here we were blasting with 20-25 knots of breeze up the stern. How well we were doing against the Farr boats was anyone's guess, but we were pretty happy with our progress and with the way *Lion* lifted her skirts with the puffs.

As we approached the Doldrums, the daily chat-shows between the boats provided less and less information and we weren't saying much about *Lion* either. How we got through the windless belt could dictate the outcome of this leg and

The Doldrums ahoy.

*Cole was completely at home in **Lion**'s compact, all-electric galley.*

influence the rest of the race. It was becoming increasingly difficult to get good weather maps out of Dakar despite the quality of our gear. We were getting an occasional good map, but there must have been something wrong with the Dakar transmitter. What a time for it to go on the blink! We had to rely on weather maps to help us pick the best place to cross the Doldrums. Without them, we would be flying blind and guessing hard.

Cole was doing a fantastic job in the galley and I think we were all putting on weight. He was probably the one guy on board who didn't enjoy flying fish flopping themselves on board to be presented for the cooking pot or microwave. These were usually dumped straight down the hatch above the galley, Cole more often than not in residence and in the firing line.

We'd been running just as hard and as quickly as the Farr boats, and that was encouraging news. *UBS* was still 123 miles ahead as we passed abeam of Dakar on the western extremity of the Bulge of Africa. *Atlantic Privateer* was cutting the corner and was nearly abeam to the east of us. She was doing the same runs as us but was gambling heavily on a more direct course closer to the African coast. *Drum* was 75 miles astern of us and about 60 miles further inshore.

Interestingly, *UBS* had gone in too and was about 40 miles closer to the coast than *Lion,* which was now the most westerly boat in the fleet. The positioning for the Doldrums had started and for the time being I was quite happy with where we were. I didn't like the inshore prospects of grinding to a halt earlier. Although *Atlantic Privateer* had reported doing bursts of 29 knots whereas our best speed was 20 knots, we were covering the same distance, which indicated we had more consistent wind further out to sea. We were tickled pink that the length advantage the other maxis

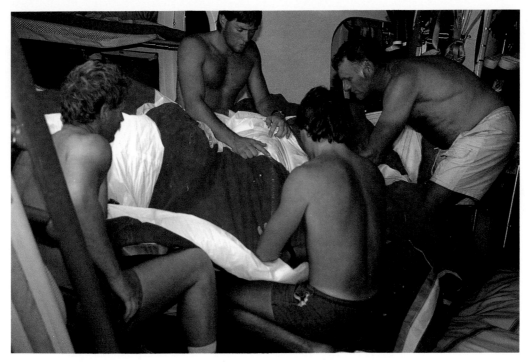

The sailmakers are kept busy with running repairs — with advice from Vonny.

enjoyed had yet to prove a factor. *Lion* was holding them in their conditions and we still had the upwind thrash through the south-east trades to come, once through the Doldrums.

On October 10, soon after midday, the wind had been getting lighter and the temperatures hotter. Just before lunch, we looked across to the west and there was *NZI*. After 12 days of hard racing, we were almost within spitting distance of one another. She must have scored by going even further to sea than *Lion* in the last 24 hours because she'd put 30-40 miles on us while we had been holding *Atlantic Privateer* and catching *UBS* in a hurry. Fehlmann was now only 95 miles ahead. *Cote D'Or*, following the same track as *Atlantic Privateer*, in on the African coast, had closed to 120 miles astern. Kuttel and Tabarly clearly were hoping to whistle straight through by following the coast around the Bulge and not getting held up by the Doldrums.

Drum was 70 miles astern of *Lion*, following the same course further out to sea, tracking down between 20 degrees and 21 degrees West. She had reported three days of north-east tradewinds of up to 38 knots true, and had done a 24-hour run of 301 miles, which explained how she had closed in on the leading group again. The boats that had got it wrong in the Bay of Biscay and down the Portuguese coast were now right back in the hunt. At the halfway mark in the leg it was still anyone's race, even though *UBS* had a slight edge.

We finally struck the Doldrums early on October 12, and they were relatively kind to us. We were totally becalmed for a maximum of only two hours. The rest of the time we made good speed, under spinnaker and going in the right direction, so that our worst day's run was a fantastic 160 miles. Thirty-six hours after going in, we were out and in the clear and the noon sched on October 13 showed us to have

Not a zephyr in sight to break the Doldrum monotony.

a comfortable lead on the rest of the fleet, although nobody was sure of *NZI*'s position. Taylor was having power problems. He'd decided not to divert to the Canaries for generator parts after he learned that he would have to drop anchor in a bay or go into port to take those parts aboard. So now he couldn't, or wouldn't, communicate and his on-board Argos satellite transmitter had failed too. Although *Atlantic Privateer* had heard Taylor talking to Portishead radio back in England, we couldn't even raise him on VHF Channel 16 when we had had him in sight. There were already grumblings through the fleet about this situation and about Taylor's not taking his turn as fleet radio boat.

Our best guess was that *NZI* was still very close to us, which meant that the two New Zealand boats had a lead of nearly 15 miles on *Atlantic Privateer*, 60 miles on *UBS*, which had really come a cropper, 70 miles on *Drum* and 120 miles on *Cote D'Or*. To celebrate clearing the Doldrums, the log read: 'Breeze going south-west and sky starting to clear. Changed from No. 1 light genoa to No. 1 medium. Yippee. Get your ya yas out, keep your timber limber and don't let your meatloaf.'

The jubilation was a little premature, however. We were hard on the wind, switching between the No. 1 medium genoa and the No. 2, for a few hours and thought we were on our way. But the Doldrums moved south and gobbled us up again. We went through three days of this, the crew working hard with the sail changes to match the fluctuations in the wind. The boats further inshore gained on us for a while but we were still in the lead, subject to where Taylor and *NZI* were. Skip Novak, on *Drum*, was preparing to protest about *NZI*'s not taking her turn as duty radio boat while apparently having enough power to transmit back to Auckland through Portishead radio to service sponsors' requirements. But for the meantime we could only take a punt as to *NZI*'s whereabouts.

Atlantic Privateer had scored in on the Liberian coast, coming out with a south-westerly while we were getting more of a southerly. She had been down the mine a couple of days back, but now she was only 15-20 miles behind us in terms of distance to Cape Town, although we were the best part of 200 miles apart from east to west. *UBS* was 30-35 miles astern on a middle course, while *Drum* was out where we were, but 55 miles astern. We still had the weather berth on the fleet, however, and spirits on board were high.

Nearly through the windless belt, so Tony gets in some practice for tougher times ahead.

Mainsail maintenance before the south-east trades.

Out at last and the Doldrums make a welcome sight — astern.

The big decision now was when to commit to port tack and start to make southing as quickly as possible. We'd been going in towards the African coast on starboard tack for more than 24 hours, as had everyone else in the leading group, but the port tack had been looking better all the time, and at 1920 hours on the 16th we made our move. Immediately it looked good. We were heading almost due south and churning off the miles. From the books I had on board, I noted that *Flyer* had gone 180 miles further to the east than where we were before she tacked on to port, but we would cross her track by the evening of the 17th, which was an indication of how favourable the port tack was for us on this occasion. We crossed the equator at 2325 hours the same day, at 10 degrees 30 minutes West, so it was a double occasion.

The breeze stayed east of south for the next 48 hours and freshened to the stage where we were down to the No. 3 genoa and reefing the mainsail. *Lion* was jumping and holding her lead on the boats which had continued on starboard tack well to the east of the rhumbline.

Then the wind shifted to the north-north-east — extraordinary when one was in the south-east trades belt. Part of the reason probably was that the high pressure system which normally dominates the South Atlantic was well to the east of its customary position, close in to the coast of southern Africa. The weather maps from Pretoria also showed that there was a low coming off the South American continent which might provide a funnel effect between it and the high which was sitting to the east of St Helena. I was quite happy to keep heading more to the south than directly towards Cape Town. There was always the danger of running smack into the high and stalling. The recognised approach to the Cape of Good Hope was to make

King Neptune comes aboard to demand his dues . . . looks a bit like Vonny in drag.

southing as quickly as possible and then curve in behind the high with the prospect of fresh tailwinds.

By this stage we had *NZI* plotted just to the west of us. It seemed she had tacked on to port a little earlier, and now we were clearly the two furthest west in the fleet, although *Drum* was following a similar course. *UBS* was recovering again on a course between ours and those of *Atlantic Privateer* and *Cote D'Or,* which were a long way to the east. The fleet plot on the chart was highly interesting with six maxis spread out in a line across the ocean with not much difference really in the distances they had to travel to Cape Town. Who had got it right — ourselves out to the west, following the traditional route, or the boats gambling on a course well to the east of the norm?

We got part of the answer almost immediately. On the night of October 23, after 25 days at sea, we ran into 12 hours of almost complete calm. The breeze had been switching crazily from the north-west to the south-east, and then it died almost completely. It was worse than the Doldrums, and I had an awful feeling that it was a private parking lot. The next day we listened gloomily to the radio to find that some of the other boats had done 100 miles more than us in the last 24 hours. *Atlantic Privateer* was now 120 miles closer to Cape Town, although still well to the east. While we were struggling to make 105 miles to the south, *Cote D'Or,* which was now heading due south down the Atlantic, had covered 200 miles. *Drum* had caught and passed us, and *UBS* had gained 35-40 miles on *Lion.* It was a really low blow. The only solace was that we'd sighted *NZI* on the 24th. She'd been 20 miles ahead according to the position reports on the 23rd — Taylor was finally making his location known — but we'd pulled him in all through the night until by dawn we had him in sight. By late evening we had him mast down on the horizon to the south of us.

The gale starts to build . . . and turns life into a heaving hell.

The lead had changed again, but there was no use our getting down in the dumps about the fact that it had been our turn to suffer. There was still a long way to go to Cape Town and much could yet happen. The log pointed out that 'the opera isn't over until the fat lady sings'. The entries for October 24 noted: 'NZI in sight once again, four miles ahead on our bow,' then 'We've now rolled NZI to leeward, she's going out the back door like you would not believe. Seems to be on her way to Cape Horn.' As if to remind everyone that the leg was nearing a close, there came the final entry: 'The fat lady has entered the hall.'

Our run for the 24 hours was a demoralising 105 miles. We improved that to 173 miles in the next 24 hours but the wind was still waffly and we were getting frustrated even though we were still close to NZI, having our own private match-race out in the middle of the South Atlantic.

The breeze was up and down all through October 25 and we had NZI in view all day on our starboard quarter. The log reminded everyone: 'The fat lady is in her changing room,' then noticed that 'there's a funny sea running now, big swell with chop running in opposite direction. Hard to steer.' There was something going on ahead of us that was pushing up a big sea in our path.

Conditions freshened a little on the 26th, but we still couldn't work out where the sea was coming from. NZI was fine on the starboard bow and we had her in sight for the next 24 hours as the breeze at last began to gain in strength. It built slowly through the 28th until by nightfall we had 30 knots across the deck and the sea was 'Tatapatchish'. We'd tacked on to starboard and were heading straight for Cape Town where, we heard by radio, it was blowing 60 knots plus. Now we knew where all the rubbish was coming from.

On the 29th the sea was rough to say the least, even though we still only had winds of mostly 20-25 knots. We'd done 200 miles noon to noon but were having to hold Lion back a bit. She'd already leapt out of two particularly big and backless waves to land with a real crunch on the other side. Under No. 5 jib and double-reefed mainsail, we were still doing eight knots close-hauled.

We lost track of NZI late on the 27th. She seemed to be faster than Lion on the wind in the fresh stuff, although she couldn't point as high. But we appeared to be a lot faster than her in the light, so it was a swings-and-roundabouts situation. Now we heard on the radio that she had broken her main halyard and ripped her mainsail. Her crew couldn't get a new main halyard reeved until the sea died down a bit, and there wasn't much hope of that according to the weather maps.

The South Atlantic High, much lower down and further east than usual, was piling the isobars up against the southern African continent near Cape Town. Gale-force southerlies were being spun off into the path of the maxis. But the wind wasn't the real problem, more the fact that it was blowing across the prevailing south-westerly ground swell from the Southern Ocean to produce an evil, steep sea for up to 1000 miles off the coast. This combination proved disastrous for the maxi division. Drum was the first to succumb. The continuous pounding on starboard tack as she headed for the African coast proved too much for her construction and she began to delaminate through a lengthy strip of her for'ard port sections. In other words, the two skins of Kevlar in her hull had sheered away from the honeycombed core material that was the meat in the sandwich. The 'meat' was being ground into powder by friction as the hull moved leaving two unsupported skins of flexible fibreglass in a part of the boat which was taking a fearful pounding as Drum ploughed through the

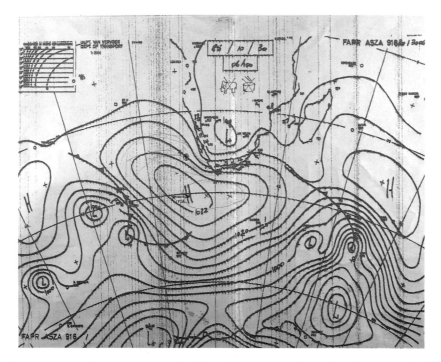

*The weather situation as the maxis approached Cape Town, as per the on-board map received by **Lion**'s satellite facsimile receiver. The strong winds were generated by funnelling between the South Atlantic High, which was to the south and east of its normal position, and the low pressure system over South Africa.*

big seas. Skip Novak had little option. He squared away downwind, reduced sail and started for the port of Luderitz in Namibia (South-West Africa), 480 miles up the coast from Cape Town, to assess the full extent of the damage.

Drum had been 600 miles from the finish when her situation became acute. Three hours later, from a similar position to *Drum*'s, *Cote D'Or* reported that she too was delaminating in the port sections forward of the mast, the area of the boat which was taking most of the punishment as she came out of the waves and landed in the troughs. Tabarly had tacked on to port and headed almost due south while he took stock of his predicament. *NZI* was continuing after her riggers had courageously spent a torturous time at the top of the mast reeving a new halyard so that the spare Kevlar main could be hoisted.

That night, race director Rear Admiral Charles Williams, in Cape Town, alerted the South African Navy and other race yachts in the vicinity that he had three maxis with problems, two of them serious. There was no relief. It was blowing so hard in Cape Town that people were having to use ropes to cross intersections in the downtown part of the city, and now we were copping winds of greater strength and even more vicious seas.

Atlantic Privateer was the next to fall, at a time when she was just a day from the finish and a long way in the lead for line honours. Kuttel radioed in to report that part of his starboard rigging had failed and the mast had gone overboard. Like *Drum*, he was running with the now full gale and heading for Luderitz. *NZI* struck more trouble soon afterwards. Her port cap shroud tore away from the mast and, unsupported, the top of the spar had kinked and was leaning over to port at an alarming angle.

This left just two maxis still performing — UBS and Lion — and we both had our problems. Fehlmann was down to trisail and small jib, and nursing UBS. He couldn't reef his mainsail deeply enough to get rid of sufficient area in the blow so he'd taken it down. Now he faced the problem of getting it up again if the wind eased. That wouldn't be easy in the seaway that was running. On Lion, we were down to No. 5 jib and three reefs in the main. We were taking a hammering but the boat was going like a rocket. The boys nicknamed her 'The Urban Wave Destroyer' because she just kept on trucking despite seas that were so steep, you felt you would slide back down the face of them.

We were threading a path through the worst of those seas, trying to smooth out the ride a bit and keep the boat from pounding too hard. This was when we discovered the good and the not-so-good rough weather helmsman. Ralph Lucas, for instance, seemed to have a knack of staying on the smooth parts of the 'road', but Goddy Cray found every single pothole. It may have been that one helmsman would come on when the seas evened out for a while and another would inherit the wheel when it was decidedly rough. Low Life Quilter earned himself the title 'Earthquake' with the most horrifying crunch of the whole deal.

It was the Sydney-Hobart all over again — not as much wind, but seas just as punishing. Still, the only serious concern aboard Lion was on the weather rail where the smokers in the crew were in dire straits. Desperately low on matches, they resorted to keeping one cigarette alight 24 hours a day, not an easy task the way Lion was chucking the water about. We pounded on into what should have been our last night at sea on this leg, and a wonderfully wild and moonlit night it was. I was enjoying a spell on the wheel when the Doc pointed to the mainsail. He could see the moon through the cloth. Before we could do anything, the sail split right across. We sounded the emergency alarm to summon all hands for a mainsail change. By this stage the flogging and torn mainsail had really given up the ghost, tearing right up the seam between the Dacron cloth and the Kevlar. With a great deal of care, because Lion was still doing eight knots through 25-foot breaking seas, we lowered the mainboom to the deck and rolled the now-ruined sail into a manageable unit.

There was nothing else to do but dump it over the side once we'd salvaged

The calm after the storm, with Cape Town in sight and the cloth spread on The Table.

the battens and any fittings that would be useful again. It wasn't an easy decision. A replacement would cost $30,000. But the sailmakers were adamant that the Kevlar had had it and the sail was irreparable. So we cut it from the boom and eased it over the side. Within 70 minutes of the Doc noticing the start of our problem, we were pedal to the metal again with the replacement Dacron main triple-reefed and *Lion* back up to nine knots.

The gale abated with almost indecent haste, leaving us to struggle the remaining miles into Table Bay in light and variable winds with frustrating patches of calm. *UBS* was going to beat us by about 16 hours but there was nothing we could do as we ghosted towards Robben Island, in the mouth of Table Bay, striving to keep the spinnaker full in the lightest of airs.

At first light, close in on the shore of Robben Island where Nelson Mandela was incarcerated, we made out the lines of a tug which was coming to meet us. Sarah-Jane was waving madly and there were Pippa, Jappi's wife, Ginny, and Ralph's wife, Heather, along with Peter Montgomery and Alan Sefton. It would be another couple of hours before we could greet them properly, but it was great to see some friendly and very familiar faces after what we had just been through.

Finally, at 0706 hours local time on November 2, having been at sea for 34 days 17 hours 46 minutes since leaving Portsmouth on September 28, we crossed the finish line. *UBS* had beaten us by 16 hours 7 minutes and it was clear that the leg, on handicap, was going to be a small-boat bonanza, as they were coming in only a couple of days behind us after a dream run down the Atlantic, missing out on the blow completely.

But *Lion* had proved herself again. As the casualties began to limp in — both *Cote D'Or* and *Drum* had resumed course to Cape Town as soon as conditions had improved, and *NZI* had nursed her damaged rig in — there were no jibes about *Lion's* being 'off the pace' or 'too heavy'. My lot wouldn't have swapped their vessel for anything else in the fleet at that stage and there were any number among the opposition who would have been happy to change places with them.

LEG 1: PORTSMOUTH-CAPE TOWN

Elapsed Time		Corrected Time	
	Days/Hrs Min/Sec		Days/Hrs Min/Sec
1. UBS Switzerland	34.01.39.19	1. L'Esprit D'Equipe	32.07.07.47
2. Lion New Zealand	34.17.46.47	2. Philips Innovator	32.18.38.09
3. Cote D'Or	34.23.28.26	3. Fazer Finland	32.23.15.55
4. NZI Enterprise	35.09.06.42	4. UBS Switzerland	33.23.05.31
5. Fazer Finland	36.10.33.09	5. Fortuna Lights	34.08.09.55
6. Philips Innovator	36.12.28.11	6. Lion New Zealand	34.11.45.25
7. Drum England	36.16.44.23	7. Cote D'Or	34.14.49.27
8. L'Esprit D'Equipe	37.13.41.25	8. NZI Enterprise	35.09.06.42
9. Fortuna Lights	38.18.46.48	9. Shadow of Switzerland	36.09.16.08
10. Norsk Data GB	39.15.09.53	10. Rucanor Tristar	36.13.19.49
11. Rucanor Tristar	42.02.10.04	11. Drum England	36.13.44.48
12. Shadow of Switzerland	43.06.12.40	12. Norsk Data GB	39.02.31.20
13. Equity And Law	47.18.23.05	13. Equity And Law	41.20.13.22
14. SAS Baia Viking	51.18.15.56	14. SAS Baia Viking	44.22.06.47
15. Atlantic Privateer	Did not finish	15. Atlantic Privateer	Did not finish

---

Table Mountain provides a magnificent backdrop to **Lion**'s dawn arrival.

7. Southern Ocean Sleighrides?

The Cape Town scene as the fleet straggled in should have provided the Royal Naval Sailing Association with much food for thought on where its race was headed. The Whitbread dock, near the Royal Cape Yacht Club, resembled the pit area after a stockcar demolition derby. One maxi, *Atlantic Privateer,* had been dismasted. Another had a bend in its mast that was severe enough to render the rig useless. Two others were in need of major constructional repair after being in danger of breaking up. That represented a casualty rate of 60 percent among the maxis, and there were serious doubts whether three of the big boats could continue the race. The smaller yachts had not encountered conditions anything like those which had decimated the big guns, but there was no reason to believe that they would have escaped a similarly alarming damage list if they had.

Yet the truth of the matter was that a well-found Round the World race fleet should have taken the four-day gale coming into Cape Town in its stride. Sure, it had been nasty and some of the seas were amongst the worst one would like to encounter. But it wasn't severe enough to wreak the havoc that it did among boats which had supposedly been purpose-built to handle such weather conditions.

Kuttel had made a valiant effort to keep *Atlantic Privateer* in the race, organising to Luderitz a jury rig, fabricated from steel steam pipes, for her arrival under motor. Within hours his crew had rigged the stove-pipe mast and *Atlantic Privateer* was back to sea, motoring and then sailing towards the spot where she'd stopped racing when her original rig fell over. Kuttel's plan was to go back to that point and then resume the leg to Cape Town, which he in fact was not permitted to do under the rules of the race. As soon as he used his motor he was automatically disqualified from the leg.

But disaster struck less than 30 minutes after the crew bent sail on to their unusual spar. The pipe wasn't up to the job and *Atlantic Privateer,* for the second time in as many days, was mastless. On this occasion she motored to Cape Town, her campaign in ruins. Kuttel thought of quitting and there was a falling out with his sailing master, David Bongers, who had continued to load sail on and press the yacht when she had the leg won and could have been nursed through the remainder of the blow.

Finally, Kuttel secured a replacement mast — which was being built in Cape Town for a boat of similar size — and elected to continue, without Bongers, even though he could win individual leg honours only.

One had to feel for Skip Novak. Having broken all sorts of records to resurrect *Drum* after her Fastnet race capsize, there he was with another rebuilding job to do and one which, in its own way, was every bit as serious as the last. Charles Williams and the RNSA quite correctly appointed an independent expert to assess *Drum*'s damage and report whether satisfactory repairs were possible. It had transpired that *Drum*'s problems were not restricted to the topside panels which had delaminated. Her floor was also flexing under the strains imposed by the keel.

Novak flew in Adrian Thompson, from England, the man who had engineered *Drum*'s construction, and Butch Dalrymple-Smith, from the Holland office, to investigate the alternatives. They all agreed that *Drum* could be rebuilt and strengthened, but it was going to take a major effort with the restart scheduled for December 4, only three weeks hence. Novak would succeed and *Drum* would be there for the departure to Auckland, but one wondered what the crew would be thinking as they headed down into the Southern Ocean with a yacht that was acquiring a 'jinxed' reputation.

Cote D'Or's damage was not quite as extensive, but the repairs required the same overall approach and expert approval. Tabarly wasn't stopping there, however. He was concerned with the boat's bow-down tendencies which verged on dangerous in fresher conditions. So he was replacing *Cote D'Or*'s keel with a new bulbed appendage which would shift the centre of balance further aft and make *Cote D'Or* a different proposition altogether downwind.

This posed a dilemma for the race committee as no such alterations were allowed once the race had started. Tabarly would be disqualified if he did as he intended, or he would have to withdraw from leg one and restart his race from Cape Town. A compromise was reached with *Cote D'Or* being given a 97-hour time penalty for the race, but her performance in leg one would still count. Effectively, however, *Cote D'Or* was out of contention for all but individual leg honours.

NZI Enterprise had the fairly simple job of replacing the mast. They had built a spare to provide for this possibility and that mast was already being prepared for air freight to Cape Town, before *NZI* had crossed the Cape Town finish-line. Taylor

Ian Sims' farm near Stellenbosch was a perfect place to relax with nary a boat in sight.

Aran's container base in Cape Town provided everything needed for the in-port refit.

was fortunate to have campaign manager Max Jones on the spot in South Africa to deal promptly with the situation. Even so, with the inevitable hitches inherent in sending halfway around the world an item as big and as awkward to load as a maxi mast, it was a lengthy job and the spar finally went in the boat just a couple of days before the restart. The *NZI* crew spent some of the waiting-time repairing some cracked frames and stiffening the transom which was racking under runner backstay loads.

Even Fehlmann had his mast out to attend to cracking around the inboard spreader-ends. On *Lion,* there was little to do except running maintenance. Within four days of our arrival, and after the crew had enjoyed the much anticipated 'few coldies' at the yacht club bar — for 'few' read 'many' and toss in a large quantity of dark rum and coke too — the boat had been scrubbed out from stem to stern, checks and jobs had been completed, and we were about ready to go again but for the loading of fresh food supplies. This gave everyone the chance to take a couple of weeks away from the yacht and they set off in groups to explore the country on motorbikes or take trips to game parks.

Dalts was down in the dumps for the first few days. He'd arrived in Cape Town ready to roar, but was quickly subdued by a 'Dear John' letter from his girlfriend. Probably fortunately for him, although it might not have seemed so at the time, the rest of the crew afforded him no sympathy whatsoever and, in the style that was all their own, ribbed him mercilessly until he was forced to buck up and join in the fun.

Dalts was also known as 'No Neck', a nickname which described his appearance when in hard training for power-lifting competitions. He also worked for Feltex Ropes (now Kinnears) in Auckland, selling mostly their racing lines to the yachting trade. So he immediately copped jibes like 'Dalt tried to hang himself last night, but he couldn't find his neck' and 'Dalts tried to hang himself again last night but the Feltex rope broke'.

Pippa, Sarah-Jane and I were the guests of Ian Sims and his wife, Joanne, for the duration of our stay in Cape Town and, as in the 1981-82 race, they were superb hosts. Ian, a New Zealander, was head of B.P. Southern Africa and very well versed in the intricacies and developments on that troubled continent. I spent many a long hour discussing the situation with him and found that, contrary to what we might be led to believe in the outside world, much was being done to change the system of apartheid in South Africa and to drastically improve the lot of the black man.

Major companies like B.P. were heavily involved in retraining and rehousing programmes, providing good job prospects and striving to integrate the blacks into the work force with equal opportunity. But South Africa's is not simply a black versus white problem, and nor are the solutions for that beautiful country as simple as some in the outside world would like to believe. It will take patience and understanding, on all sides, to unravel the complexities of 300 years of history and tradition.

One couldn't help but feel apprehensive for the future of the country, particularly with increasing pressure for sanctions and the continuing campaign to sever all sporting contacts with South Africa. The approaches, I feared, fail to understand the very nature of the Boer whose generations of ancestors settled what was originally a wild and mostly empty land. I never had seen any sense in stand-off tactics, anyway. Communication and education are, after all, two of the bedrocks of modern civilisation.

I would have liked more time to explore the country and its problems because, the way things were heading, this surely would be the last time the Whitbread race would call at Cape Town, in the forseeable future anyway. But the days and weeks

Here we go again.

flew by until suddenly the restart was upon us.

The wind was light and from the west as we went to the line in Table Bay at 1100 hours on Wednesday, December 4. We were going home, hopefully for New Year's Eve. The first five boats across the finish-line in Cape Town had broken *Flyer's* record for that leg — *UBS Switzerland* clipping 2 days 9 hours off *Flyer's* 1981-82 time — and if we could maintain the same sort of improvement through the Southern Ocean, we could be in Auckland by December 31. What a party that would make!

I didn't start us out very well, however, getting *Lion* tangled up in a port-starboard protest incident with *UBS,* with me in the wrong. It took a while to get moving, but we passed Cape Point by mid-afternoon compared to late the following morning in *Ceramco* four years ago. *NZI* and *UBS* led past the Cape of Good Hope, just ahead of *Atlantic Privateer, Lion, Cote D'Or* and *Drum* — all within sight of one another and travelling fast into a big, lumpy sea.

The wind gradually backed through the east to the north-east and then north-west, and then finally west to send us trucking along at 11 knots on course for the Southern Ocean under full main, the 1.5oz reacher and the big boy sail in moderate seas, with *NZI* in sight ahead and *Drum* to windward but astern. Our course was between 150 degrees and 160 degrees magnetic which, on a great circle route, would take us close to the Kerguelen Islands.

The crew didn't take long to settle down to the routine and the repartee between the two watches was unabated. Dalts was still catching it because of his 'Dear John' letter, but now the jibes were about his having spent Rand 100 on the last night in Cape Town talking to his girlfriend who was working in the United States. It appeared

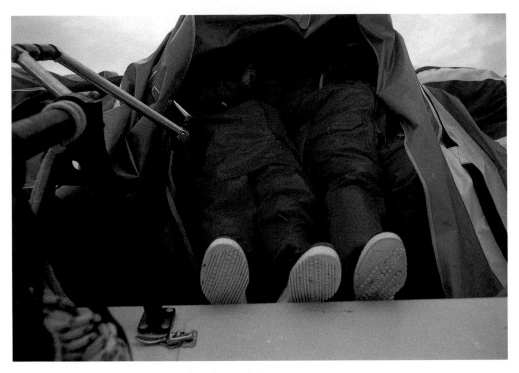

The warmer weather was too good to last and the Southern Ocean's ahead.

everything was back on again, much to the disgust of the rest of the crew. Everyone was a little tensed up, anticipating some wild downwind rides in the days to come, but day three at sea was spent loafing along under spinnaker, with *Drum* tight on our stern, doing three knots at best.

That evening, though, the breeze came ahead from the south-west and freshened quickly. Was this it, we thought, as *Lion* picked up speed under a sometimes reefed main, staysail and jib top. But no, Hughie was only teasing us. Soon we were changing back up through the wardrobe until we were drifting again under full main and windseeker headsail.

While we were struggling, the Farr boats had snuck away to the south of us and were 50 miles ahead. They obviously hadn't struck as much light stuff as we had, but on day five, December 8, the wind freshened swiftly again, this time from the north-east, and *Lion* picked up speed, tight-reaching with her rail under. Maybe we'd got this one first, being a little further north, and we would make up lost ground. *Atlantic Privateer* was heading south as quickly as possible, but *NZI* and *Drum* were on a course only slightly south of *Lion*'s.

I hadn't yet decided whether we would hold up high or dive off down into the Southern Ocean with its possibility of ice. The weather in the next few days would dictate that decision. For the moment though it was blowing hard enough to keep us happy, even though it was ahead of the beam and making life on the windward rail somewhat miserable.

The weather was getting cooler and more clothing started to appear for the first

Hardly master blaster stuff.

Baby, it's cold outside . . . Vonny ready to go on deck.

time since leaving England. Raw Meat had everyone in stitches when he dug into his kit to produce a knitted item which turned out to be a 'Willie Warmer', otherwise known as a 'Peter Heater'. He was quite disgusted when he tried it on and found that it was about three sizes too big and disappeared for'ard muttering that his mother must have knitted it for an elephant. He planned to line the thing with newspaper, but I don't think he quite got around to it.

Again the wind died. We had been blasting along with up to 35 knots of true wind still ahead of the beam, until the breeze suddenly clocked from the north-east then to the north-west and started to lighten until we were up to the .75 kite and full main. The log commentary for December 10 said it all: 'This is not as per the brochures — Simon just did a 360. Where's the wind?'

We were now a week out from Cape Town and by this time in *Ceramco* we had been master-blasting, chasing *Flyer* through the Southern Ocean on some wildly exciting downwind rides. We'd lost out to the boats to the north of us and to the south, and the log complained: 'We had our own, our very own, private, bloody calm AGAIN today. F... it.' But, as usual at sea, there was a bit of give-and-take. As we slid through between Prince Edward Island and Marion Island, we learned by radio that we had pulled *NZI* and *UBS* back, and that *Cote D'Or*, well to the north, had slowed right up. The only boat which had pulled away from everyone was *Atlantic Privateer*. This meant that a more southerly course was better but we were heading

No place like a warm bunk with a good book . . . Ed relaxes off watch.

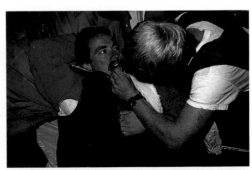

A tooth filling for Shoeby is all part of a day's work for the Doc.

Everyone wants to be the chef in weather like this.

You grab what sleep you can where you can — the skipper dozes in the navigatorium.

due east on port gybe at the time, and to gybe over to go further south would not have been a smart move. We would have been heading due south at a big angle away from the direction in which we wanted to go.

There's a permanently manned South African weather station on Marion Island, but we only got a murky glimpse of Prince Edward Island as we went by, and the crew was sceptical about that sighting. The log read: 'Passed (according to our tour leader) between two islands this morning. They were not seen by watch members and there have been mutterings about (a) the tour leader's integrity and (b) the tour leader's sanity.'

Late that afternoon we did it again — we found another calm patch. We'd been feeling pretty pleased with the recovery job we'd done on NZI and UBS, and the miles we'd put on Cote D'Or. But then we ran out of wind completely, as the ocean became glassy calm. We hoped the situation was pretty general as we sat there going nowhere until the breeze filled back in from the south-east at 16-18 knots. Then we heard the bad news. Our flat spot had been a private affair. Drum had been only 15 or 16 miles to the north of us but had sailed on by, and in a 12-hour period had put 60 miles on Lion.

That was enough. We'd been caught out several times by sailing the middle course in what were clearly very unusual conditions for this part of the ocean. Now we would get down south in search of some favourable wind. The plan was to continue on down to around 55 degrees South, then level out and play the weather systems as they came through. It was no good staying where we were as the wind was all over the place, and sometimes there wasn't any at all.

So down we went in a bid to get below the opposition and lift out underneath them. The price, of course, was significantly colder temperatures. The water was 2.3 degrees Celsius and the air was no warmer. The log observed: 'On the wind again, a wonderfully enriching experience with 2 degrees C. temperatures and probably a 10 degree wind chill factor. It must be cold. It now takes two men to make the tea. Food has run out, exhausted. Captain Oates has just gone outside, said he could be some time. Bitterly cold.'

It started to snow on December 12 and L'Esprit D'Equipe reported sighting a 300-metre-long iceberg, quite some way to the north of us. We'd have to keep our eyes peeled. As we passed 50 degrees South and then 52 degrees South, on Black Friday, December 13, the log noted: 'Whale passed across our bow, heading north (more sensible than us). Aran happy to know that his relatives are nearby.'

In these near zero temperatures people's minds tend to work a little slower than usual and we were taking care with sail changes on deck. But the cold only seemed to heighten the humour. The Doc was wandering around the boat asking people if they'd seen his elephant, and he and Combo posted notices all over the boat to warn that they had laid a land mine here or poison there. I don't know what they were hoping to catch.

By late on December 14 we were down to 53 degrees 36 minutes South, and it looked like our decision was going to pay handsome dividends. We were 'honking' under chicken chute (heavy, flat-cut running spinnaker) in 30 knots of wind. I had a spell on the wheel and got a burst of 21.6 knots, Lion's best yet. The swell was long, so ideal for surfing. Cote D'Or was now 500 miles to the north of us — she at 45 degrees South and Lion at 53 degrees 30 minutes South. NZI and Drum were only just ahead of us, albeit a bit further north, and UBS wasn't too far away from them. The only boat which continued to hold her own against us was *Atlantic Privateer*.

Still, it was all very close after 11 days at sea and there was still a long way to go. We'd just done our best noon to noon run, 290 miles in what were fairly average conditions, which told us that 300-mile days would be easy with just a few knots more wind. *NZI* reported in to say she had broken a spinnaker pole and wrapped the kite around the headfoil, but she'd still managed a good day's run.

December 17 started well. The barometer was down to 967 millibars and it was blowing 30 knots, but squally. *Lion* was blasting along as we rang the changes from chicken chute to No. 3 jib top and back up the range. At about 1900 hours we decided to try the storm spinnaker. We'd never had much luck with that sail, it always seemed to press the bow down, but maybe we'd been setting it up wrong. We hauled it up and took off at 19 knots. The boat was controllable but she was burying her bow coming down the seas. *Lion* didn't stop either, so we were charging into the backs of waves like a submarine. We lasted 20 minutes like that, with the boatspeed never dropping below 15 knots. It was exhilarating stuff, but it was also getting risky. So we changed back to the chicken chute.

We were now down to 54 degrees 34 minutes South with air and water temperatures hovering around zero. The guys certainly knew now what the Southern Ocean was all about. *Lion* was about 3900 miles from Auckland and in a few days we would be 'under' Australia but a long, long way south of the great arid land. We were in good shape, still the furthest south in the fleet, and covering less distance compared to the boats further north. Now all we needed was a bit of yachties' luck for a change.

The log enquired: 'Will Mike Quilter stick to his word — "I'd rather drink piss with my mates than get married" and will Kevin Basil Barry Shoebridge's aunty (?!!?) in South Africa be at home when he calls?' Shoeby was coming in for a lot of stick about his romance with a woman called Lynn in South Africa. He made the fatal mistake of calling her by radio telephone from the boat. The log was littered with ribald references to the 'romance'. One entry lamented: 'Shoeby talked to Lynn today. She had the gall to say over the phone "I miss you!" What has happened to our star performer with the ladies?'

Fuzz was alternatively known as 'Dog'. In Cape Town, he'd acquired, as a joke, a veterinary health certificate, all properly filled out and signed by an authorised vet, which read: 'I hereby certify that at the request of Fuzz Dogstein (Grant Spanhake), at the Sea Point Veterinary Clinic on December 2, 1985, I have examined the animal described hereunder and it is, in my opinion, free from external parasites and communicable diseases, and emanates from a herd visibly free from such diseases and fit to travel. He was subjected to the following inoculations and tests with negative results: Rabies, distemper, cat flue, leptospirosis and New Zealand boating infections.' Fuzz Dogstein was described on the form as: 'Good looking, 5ft 8in, blue eyes, curly blond hair, good coat. Breed: pedigree New Zealand boating hound.' Now he was stuck with the nickname that went with the certificate.

Roy, meanwhile, was having real problems with the plumbing. It seemed that the outlet pipe which carried all the wastes had bent over and crimped itself so that the wastes had all been discharging into one another, back through the rubber non-return valves. Vonny, not realising this was the situation, was in the for'ard head frantically bailing the indescribable concoction that all of a sudden started pumping

*This is what we came for — high winds, big seas and a roller-coaster ride towards Auckland.
The Tasman is three days ahead and we're coming home in a hurry.*

up through the shower tray while he was using the loo. Naturally, he was dumping it back down the toilet pan and it was all pumping right back around part of the blocked system and coming up through the shower tray again. Vonny just couldn't believe he was responsible for all of that.

It reminded me of the time on *Ceramco,* not long after we left Cape Town in 1981, when we noticed a disturbing amount of water in the bottom of the boat. We started to bail, manually and with an electric bilge pump, but made no impression on the water level. The sea was coming in somewhere just as fast as we could pump it out. Vonny, on that occasion, grabbed a bucket and really went for that water, tipping his buckets down the galley sink. He didn't know it, but the exit pipe from the sink had ruptured, leaving a one-inch-diameter hole outlet valve open to the ocean, and the buckets that Vonny was emptying down the sink were pouring right back into the boat too. We shut the valve down and that was the end of the problem, but we still had to empty the boat of water. By this stage Geoff Stagg, on the helm, was getting annoyed at having to keep *Ceramco* level to let the water drain into the sump. 'What the hell you guys,' Staggy shouted, 'we're racing up here.' 'That's okay for you,' Vonny retorted, 'we're sinking down here.'

LEG 2 CAPE TOWN-AUCKLAND

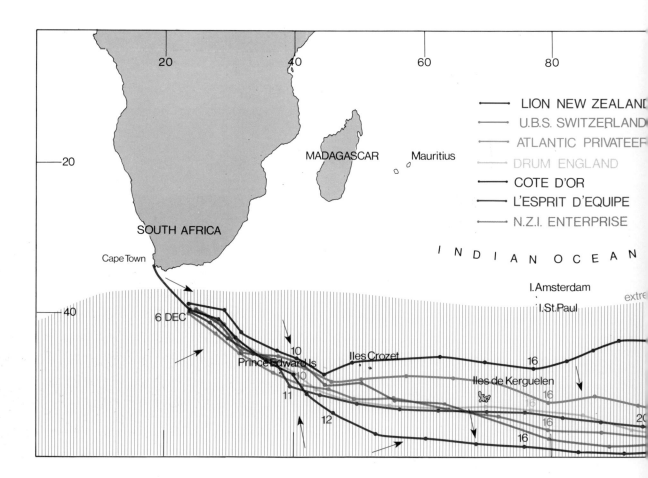

112

By December 22 we had milked all we could out of being the most southerly yacht and were starting to hurt for being down there. *NZI, Atlantic Privateer, UBS* and *Drum,* in the last couple of days, had had more consistent winds and had opened up on us, driving straight over the top of our track. In addition to that, we'd been becalmed again that morning and the boats astern were reporting little or no wind in the middle of a slow-moving low. We needed to be out of the way before that came through, whatever the cost, so we started to head north-east.

Just two days before Christmas, we weren't feeling very merry at all. The Farr boats and *Drum* were spinnaker reaching at high speed while *Lion* was still two-sail reaching in a different breeze. *Drum* was just managing to hang on to the back of the Farr designs with a mixture of good tactical calls by Skip Novak and some good luck. But *Lion,* as well as being bankrupt in the luck department, was also suffering in the predominantly tight reaching conditions. She was heavier than she should have been and she also lacked the length. She was a good yacht, without a doubt, but she did have her Achilles heel, and that heel had been exposed quite a bit on this second leg. She was able to hold her own downwind with a spinnaker on, but we'd had a total of only 24 hours of spinnaker work in three weeks since leaving Cape Town. The rest of it was two-sail reaching or beating and, in our case, sitting becalmed.

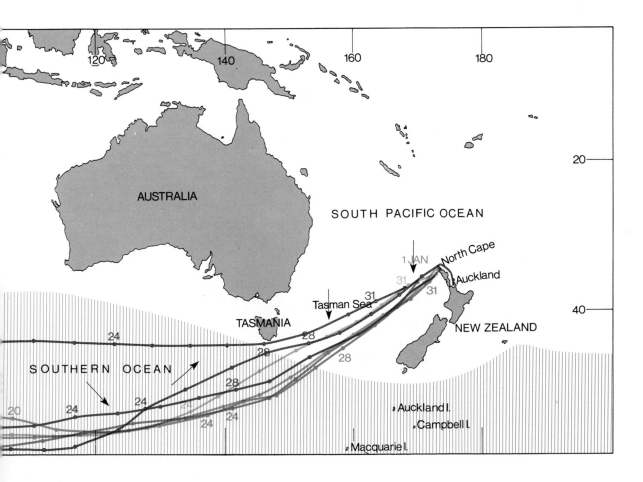

We knew it was all too good to last. The Tassy makes slow going.

At least we can enjoy the view as some compensation for lack of wind.

NZI was now 360 miles ahead of us, leading the fleet but with *Atlantic Privateer* right on her hammer. We found it staggering that we were so far behind, but there were still 2400 miles to go to Cape Reinga and a lot could happen going up the Tasman. We had to hope that the leaders would bog down in a high pressure system and give us a chance to close the gap, riding on the western edge of a front. For this reason, we were holding a bit further to the west than the leading group. It wasn't a flyer, but we were doing something positive in a bid to get among the action again. The log reminded everyone that 'the fat lady had arrived in a taxi outside the hall', but we weren't going to be in Auckland for New Year's Eve.

Christmas Day found us curving up towards the Tasman at about 49 degrees South, 134 degrees West. We had the big Air New Zealand spinnaker on and were running hard in 25-30 knots of wind, averaging 13-14 knots. The boat was handling well, and this was what we'd come for. Santa Claus visited us just before midnight with exactly the present we wanted — the news that we had put two degrees on *Drum* and were beginning to catch the front-runners.

Boxing Day was even better with the breeze holding and the sea building up to real Southern Ocean sleighride stuff. *Lion* was literally humming, the pitch of the hum increasing and decreasing with speed alterations, as she really started to do her stuff. The speedo was reading near 20 knots for hours on end and we dashed on in hot pursuit of the Farr boats. We did a 308-mile run from 1500 hours to 1500 hours, *Lion*'s best yet, and the log read: 'This is more like it — back in the fast lane. The fat lady's car has broken down so who knows what might happen.' The temperature was a balmy 11 degrees, life couldn't have been better.

The wind moderated on the 27th, but kicked in again that night so that our 24-hour run to noon on the 28th was a solid 300 miles. There was only one anxious moment and that was when Ed went out to the end of the spinnaker pole to make an adjustment to the snatch block that we were using instead of the Sparcraft parrot beak, which had fallen off. While he was out there we did a bit of a round-up and all he could do was hang on. It was the middle of the night and not a very nice place for a bloke to be at 48 degrees South, 136 degrees East. But Ed was in his special harness, hooked on to the halyard, and didn't even bat an eyelid.

Lion reeled off 900 miles in three days during this period as we cut the corner on the leading group, which was still heading more east and coming up into the Tasman in a gentler arc. I wanted to be to the west of them going into the Tasman to be first cab off the rank when any frontal systems came through. We'd put a lot of time on *Drum* and the Farr boats were a lot closer too. The winds went light on the morning of the 29th, then switched to the north-west and freshened again. *Drum* was only 85 miles ahead, having slowed down as the high that produced the wind change passed over her. Now we were keeping our fingers crossed that *NZI, Atlantic Privateer* and *UBS* would strike the same problems, in triplicate. We seemed to be moving at the same speed as the high, clinging to its coat-tails, so anything was possible.

Raw Meat had been found with a full cellophane pack of lollies in his bunk, hoarding them. As punishment, he was tied up and his mouth taped over. He was then made to watch helplessly while his lolly supply was demolished. Meat claimed the cook had given him the sweets, but BC denied that vehemently. We all knew that Meat was telling the truth, and that BC had snitched on Meat so that he could watch the fun that was bound to ensue. Meat took it all really well. He was the butt of a lot of humour at times, but he could dish it out too.

The breeze held nicely in the north-west to give us a fast two-sail reach up the Tasman in smooth water. *NZI* and *Atlantic Privateer* were having a tremendous scrap for the lead, match-racing almost, but they were being overhauled by the high and we were pulling them back fast. The log read: 'Fast sailing on a nice, clear night — must be getting close to real Kiwi joker country.'

At 2220 hours that night, the log noted: 'Whale strike. Hit him at 11.5 knots. No sign of any damage, to us anyway.' That last comment was to prove optimistic, as we would soon find out, but for the moment *Lion* didn't seem to be suffering any ill-effects from the collision. The same, I'm sure, could not be said for the whale. He, or she, had collected *Lion* at full cry and that meant, at least, a 40-ton headache. The log recorded the event as follows: 'Excerpt from NZ Herald, 31/12/85 (back page, second section): Winifred Whale, her life, like a candle in the wind, was snuffed. Sorely missed by Fuzz and Cousin Wally.' Then were listed supposed comments from various ecological movements: 'Project Jonah: A dastardly deed. RSPCA: Driver did not stop to see if animal was in pain. UN Whaling Commission: NZ is a signatory to the agreement on a total ban on whaling and this act must be condemned. Greenpeace: Exactly the sort of behaviour one would expect from Blake. Beauty Without Cruelty: Blake is a beast. USSR: NZ has now exceeded its whale quota.' A more serious addendum to those entries was: 'Rudder f..... by whale, literally.' We were getting a strange vibration through the wheel and suspected the rudder was damaged. It looked all right, but it was hard to tell by torchlight.

The next morning, New Year's Day, we heard on Radio New Zealand that, in the New Year's Honours list, our Tom Clark had become Sir Thomas Clark. It couldn't have happened to a nicer guy, one who had done so much for his country's image through business and sport.

We hove to and Fuzz went over the side to check the rudder. We indeed had problems. The fibreglass blade had been broken off by the whale when it struggled to get clear of *Lion*. We'd hit it pretty hard and must have ridden up over its back so that Jonah was struck between *Lion*'s keel and rudder. The hull had received an almighty thwack from its tail as it struggled. The rudder, far more vulnerable, must

Fuzz goes down to check the damage to our rudder.

'She's buggered mate!'

have taken a belt too. Now all that was left was titanium stock and framework plus a slender leading edge fairing that looked almost like a self-steering oar blade. We'd be all right provided the wind was for'ard of the beam and we could balance the helm through the sails. But we'd be in trouble if we had to run or reach hard downwind.

The crew formed two groups to fabricate alternative steering systems in case they were needed. The sailmakers used the doors from one of the toilet capsules and made a sock to slide them into. This in turn could be pulled over the remains of the rudder frame and tied in place. Roy, Mac D, Bob and Meat took the liferaft-locker lid and secured it to the spare spinnaker pole as a giant sweep-oar.

We hove to again for an hour, tried to get the sock, containing the two toilet doors over the rudder frame, but even with two divers, Fuzz and Goddy, in the water and using all the anchor chain we had on board to sink the new device, it proved too difficult in the sloppy seas that were running. We pulled the divers and sock back aboard and carried on, fingers crossed. Fortunately, neither system was required, but we came close to having to use the sweep as the breeze freshened from astern for the final leg down the Northland coast into Auckland. We weren't going to catch the leaders anyway. They had wriggled clear of the high, were around North Cape, and on their way down the coast as we approached Cape Reinga, struggling to lay it. But the lack of effective steering would definitely slow us down for the final stages of our journey.

Late at night on January 2, as we were rounding North Cape for the last 180-mile leg of the long journey, we listened as Peter Montgomery described, on Radio New Zealand, the finish between *Atlantic Privateer* and *NZI*. We could only be envious of the crews of those two boats because the reception must have been sensational. At a few minutes before 0100 hours on January 3, they were less than 1000 metres apart and threading their way to the Orakei finish-line through a fleet of more than 500 spectator craft. The waterfront vantage points were packed and it all sounded incredibly emotional.

Atlantic Privateer had snatched the narrowest of leads over *NZI* off the Hen and

The sailmakers fabricate a sock for the toilet door solution to our rudder problems.
The boatbuilders perfect their liferaft locker-top option.

Sail Rock to port with sweep-oar emergency steering all set to go if needed.

Rangitoto Light — and we're nearly there.

Chicken Islands, 60 miles from the line. *NZI* had closed in again, but *Atlantic Privateer* held her out to cross the line 7 minutes 20 seconds ahead. They were unbelievably close after 7010 miles of racing. *UBS* followed them in, 1 hour 54 minutes later. Another nine hours slipped by before *Drum* crossed the line in fourth spot, at 1131 hours.

We were at this stage on the verge of being out of control in fresh tailwinds, but still trying for the last ounce of speed. If we could reach Orakei by 1631 hours we would still hold out *NZI* for second place on elapsed time for the two legs to Auckland. It was going to be touch-and-go. We wiped out and ruined one spinnaker, and repeated the act losing a second as we pressed on. Then we lost a third kite in a wild broach after passing Tiri Island. With a big wind-against-tide sea in the Rangitoto Channel we had our fingers crossed that we wouldn't lose control again. Wipe-outs weren't only costly on gear, they also cost time, and time we didn't have. One final gybe off North Head, executed very cautiously, and we went for the line. It was close — but we missed the deadline by just 1 minute 4 seconds. Still, it had been an exciting way to finish and nobody could say that we hadn't given it our best shot.

With a large part of Auckland's population having been up for the best part of the night watching the Farr boats finish, we didn't expect much of a reception for *Lion*. We were, after all, a somewhat distant fifth boat home. We couldn't have been more wrong. The waterfront was crowded, and *Lion* was soon surrounded by boats as she'd entered the more sheltered confines of the inner harbour.

But the best was yet to come. As we turned into the Princes Wharf basin we were greeted by a roar of football crowd proportions. The wharves, on both sides of the basin and the foreshore, were a mass of people so that it seemed like we were entering a crowded Eden Park from the players' tunnel. We were stunned, confronted by such overwhelming and spontaneous enthusiasm, and felt awfully proud to be New Zealanders. We were quite definitely home in Real Kiwi Joker country.

One more gybe before heading for the line.

120

LEG 2: CAPE TOWN-AUCKLAND

Elapsed Time	Days/H/M/S
1. Atlantic Privateer	29.03.04.36
2. NZI Enterprise	29.03.11.56
3. UBS Switzerland	29.04.59.22
4. Drum England	29.13.31.04
5. Lion New Zealand	29.18.58.12
6. Cote D'Or	30.20.07.06
7. Philips Innovator	31.12.57.26
8. Fazer Finland	32.17.45.45
9. L'Esprit D'Equipe	34.01.59.01
10. Rucanor Tristar	34.14.23.10
11. Equity And Law	34.18.29.03
12. Fortuna Lights	35.12.04.53
13. Norsk Data GB	36.00.02.49
14. Shadow of Switzerland	41.13.35.24
15. SAS Baia Viking	44.17.37.48

Corrected Time	Days/H/M/S
1. Philips Innovator	27.17.57.25
2. L'Esprit D'Equipe	28.17.46.48
3. Equity And Law	28.18.28.36
4. Atlantic Privateer	28.22.44.04
5. Rucanor Tristar	28.23.49.27
6. UBS Switzerland	29.02.23.34
7. NZI Enterprise	29.03.11.56
8. Fazer Finland	29.05.23.40
9. Drum England	29.08.17.51
10. Lion New Zealand	29.12.52.09
11. Cote D'Or	30.18.23.24
12. Fortuna Lights	31.00.04.57
13. Shadow of Switzerland	34.14.30.24
14. Norsk Data GB	35.11.14.26
15. SAS Baia Viking	37.19.20.48

Legs 1 & 2

Elapsed Time	Days/H/M/S
1. UBS Switzerland	63.06.38.42
2. NZI Enterprise	64.12.18.38
3. Lion New Zealand	64.12.44.59
4. Cote D'Or	65.19.35.32
5. Drum England	66.06.15.27
6. Philips Innovator	68.01.25.37
7. Fazer Finland	69.04.18.54
8. L'Esprit D'Equipe	71.15.40.26
9. Fortuna Lights	74.06.51.41
10. Norsk Data GB	75.15.12.42
11. Rucanor Tristar	76.16.03.14
12. Shadow of Switzerland	84.19.48.04
13. Equity And Law	82.12.52.08
14. SAS Baia Viking	96.11.53.44
15. Atlantic Privateer	DNF Leg 1

Corrected Time	Days/H/M/S
1. Philips Innovator	60.12.35.34
2. L'Esprit D'Equipe	61.00.54.35
3. Fazer Finland	62.04.39.35
4. UBS Switzerland	63.01.29.05
5. Lion New Zealand	64.00.37.34
6. NZI Enterprise	64.12.18.38
7. Fortuna Lights	65.08.14.52
8. Cote D'Or	65.09.12.51
9. Rucanor Tristar	65.12.39.16
10. Drum England	65.22.02.39
11. Equity And Law	70.14.41.58
12. Shadow of Switzerland	70.23.46.32
13. Norsk Data GB	74.13.45.46
14. SAS Baia Viking	82.17.27.35
15. Atlantic Privateer	DNF Leg 1

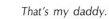

That's my daddy.

And now there came both mist and snow,
And it grew wondrous cold;
And ice, mast-high, came floating by,
As green as emerald.

Samuel Taylor Coleridge
The Rime of the Ancient Mariner

8. Who Wrote The Brochure?

The 7010-mile leg from Cape Town to Auckland traditionally has been the most rugged part of the race. This was one of the major factors in the decision to start the 1985-86 Whitbread a month later when summer had a stronger grip on the Southern Hemisphere and conditions in the Southern Ocean were a touch milder. The feeling in the fleet in Auckland, however, was that we'd been cheated.

Southern Ocean sleighrides — exhilarating downwind dashes at high speeds, in big winds and seas — are one of the attractions of the race, a vital part of its charisma. This time around, however, we'd had at best just three days of those conditions. The rest of the journey had been two-sail reaching or beating. You don't need to race around the world to do that. You can save yourself a lot of time, trouble and expense and go circuit-racing.

Thorough analysis would be needed to determine whether the vastly different conditions encountered this time were a direct result of starting a month later or whether this was simply a freak year. Still, in its own way, the trek from Cape Town had been fast enough and certainly had been tactically demanding. The first five yachts across the line — *Atlantic Privateer*, *NZI Enterprise*, *UBS Switzerland*, *Drum* and *Lion New Zealand* — had all beaten *Flyer*'s leg record of 30 days 4 hours 27 minutes 30 seconds set in the 1981-82 Whitbread.

Atlantic Privateer did the journey in 29 days 3 hours 4 minutes 36 seconds, whereas it had taken *Lion* 29 days 18 hours 58 minutes 12 seconds. Despite her problems — her topsides had again started to delaminate and she had trouble steering — *Cote D'Or* missed the record by just 16 hours. This emphasised again that the new maxis were clearly faster than anything that had raced the Whitbread before, while leg two had made the Holland boats, *Lion* and *Drum*, pay for lack of length.

In real terms, there were only three of those maxis still in the hunt for line honours around the world. *UBS*, first in Cape Town and third in Auckland, had a 1 day 5 hours margin over *NZI* and *Lion*. It was a handy lead but by no means insurmountable with still half of the race to run. *Lion*'s 1 minute 4 seconds deficit to *NZI* became 26 minutes 21 seconds when we were penalised 25 minutes 17 seconds for the port-starboard infringement against *UBS* at the start in Cape Town.

The situation was a lot better than it might have been when *NZI* and *Atlantic Privateer* dropped everyone off just before the leading group started to arc up towards the Tasman from the high latitudes. At that stage, *UBS* had been 250 miles astern of the two leaders but, like *Drum* and *Lion*, she had ridden the better winds on the back of the high pressure system moving slowly across the Tasman, and had closed to within 24 miles of *NZI* and *Atlantic Privateer* which were trapped by the high and were struggling in lighter airs. *Drum* and *Lion* had been even further off the pace but had ridden the back of the same high as *UBS* to salvation.

On corrected time, the big boats hadn't had a look-in. The 63ft Vrolijk design *Philips Innovator* took only 2 days 9 hours longer than *Atlantic Privateer* from Cape Town to Auckland and replaced the 57ft Briand design *L'Esprit D'Equipe* as overall leader after two legs. The 65ft Frers design *Fazer Finland*, a production racer-cruiser from the famous Swan stable, was doing amazingly well as the smaller yachts cashed in on conditions that weren't helping the maxis. *Fazer Finland*, owned and skippered by the delightfully self-effacing Dr Michael Berner, from Finland, was third on corrected time.

Whitbread interest in Auckland was at an all-time high, with the daily scenes at Princes Wharf almost as amazing as the welcomes. There were the estimated 20,000 people who lined the wharves to see the maxis arrive, and that figure didn't include the many thousands either out on the water or watching from the waterfront vantage points. Then there were always hundreds of people looking at the boats and enjoying the carnival atmosphere that had been created at the Whitbread Cafe with its beer garden and restaurant right alongside the arrival berths.

The nicest touch of all, however, was saved for the fleet's tail-end-Charlie *SAS Baia Viking*, a 50-footer which had been built from scrap materials by her skipper Jesper Norsk, from Denmark, and was doing the race in her own time with a very friendly male and female crew. *Baia Viking* arrived in Auckland nearly 16 days after *Atlantic Privateer*, but was still afforded a hero's welcome with dozens of spectator craft out on the water to welcome her, and a big crowd at Princes Wharf, where Harry Julian and the Auckland Harbour Board had done a tremendous job with the facilities. Auckland had again taken the Whitbread race and its contestants to its heart and

The ticker-tape parade up Queen St — a real festival occasion.

A rare sight at the McMullen & Wing dry stand area at Westhaven — five maxis in a row for maintenance.

The public interest never flagged while the fleet was in port.

the visitors were treated to New Zealand hospitality at its most generous.

If any further proof of this were needed, it was provided by the ticker-tape parade for the Whitbread crews up the country's main thoroughfare, Auckland's Queen Street. The crowds were 10-deep all the way along the route and the atmosphere was one of absolute bonhomie.

It was a lengthy but busy stopover. The restart wasn't scheduled until February 15 and we'd arrived on January 3. In that time, however, all boats had to come out of the water and take their rigs and rudders out for examination. This was compulsory at the halfway point in the long journey through the world's supposedly most unforgiving stretch of water, the Southern Ocean.

All too soon for most of us, it was time to go again. Saturday, February 15 dawned slightly overcast with a light north-easterly blowing. The Waitemata Harbour (Maori for 'sparkling waters') wasn't exactly living up to its name, but who could have seen the water anyway? Rangitoto Channel, where the restart would take place, was wall-to-wall boats, and the waterfront roads all around the harbour were jammed with vehicles, as much of Auckland sought a vantage point from which to watch the departure. There were more than 7000 boats on the water and an estimated 300,000 people lining the shoreline as New Zealand's Prime Minister David Lange fired the gun to send us away. Up above, no less than 26 helicopters and six fixed-wing aircraft, carrying television and film cameramen and the radio and print media, turned the scene into something from *Apocalypse Now*.

We were close-hauled on starboard tack for the six-mile leg out of the harbour

Lion, to leeward of the fleet, with her own entourage.

Was there ever a boat race start to match this for spectacle?

*At the **Spirit of Adventure** turn the order was **Cote D'Or**, **UBS** and **Lion**.*

to the sail-training ship *Spirit of Adventure*, which was anchored out off Auckland's East Coast Bays. I went for the uncluttered leeward end of the line and lifted out from under a couple of smaller boats in good shape. *Cote D'Or* and *UBS* were looking a threat up to weather, but *Atlantic Privateer* had been slow out of the blocks and *NZI* was trailing after tearing a headsail moments before the gun.

It was a bit like white-water rafting down one of New Zealand's major rivers as the spectator fleet homed in for a closer look, friends and families of the crew waving and shouting their farewells. In purist terms, it was the sort of scene that yachtsmen hate because the spectator wash makes it extremely difficult to attain and maintain optimum boatspeed. But who cared about that! This was a special occasion and the people of Auckland thoroughly deserved their moment. There were a few cowboys around, as there always are, but even in the crush and the rush, the spectator fleet was remarkably well-behaved and there were no major problems as the city turned on a farewell that none of us would ever forget.

At the *Spirit of Adventure, Cote D'Or* and *UBS* had worked their way over the top of us and led out of the harbour into the less-congested waters of the Hauraki Gulf. We were going to be hard on a shifty breeze all the way out to the Colville Channel some 38 miles away, so there would be a spot of really close-quarters maxi racing before we started to stretch out for the 4000-mile leg to Cape Horn.

The departure entry in the log read: 'Off to Uruguay where rum and coke costs $8 a bottle, meals and other drinks cost $9.50, a woman costs $2.50 — $20 until you can eat, drink and be merry no more. The perfect night.' It was a bit early in the piece for the boys to be thinking of the next party, but we obviously weren't going to be short on humour again on this leg.

Out in the Firth of Thames and powering along.

We reached across the Bay of Plenty in almost perfect sailing conditions — if you were on a Farr boat that is. *Lion* had been second to *Cote D'Or* through the Colville Channel but now that we'd eased sheets and were going up from reacher to our big New Zealand Shipping Line kite, *UBS* had caught and passed us, *NZI* had eased through our lee, and even *Drum*, now with Simon Le Bon aboard for the last two legs, had slipped by. The real surprise was that we were holding *Atlantic Privateer* as we passed Red Mercury Island which was owned by one of our sponsoring companies Fay, Richwhite. We were shy spinnaker-reaching on a great circle course which would take us to a predetermined point at 56 degrees South, 140 degrees West where we would level out from our dive deep into the Southern Ocean.

Approaching East Cape, the boys sighted a school of large whales up ahead and promptly called to the off-watch crew to start the generator, in a bid to scare Jonah and his mates out of our way. We didn't want another encounter like the one in the Tasman. We changed down to the heavier Air New Zealand kite as the breeze filled in, and the log observed: 'This is the only way to travel through the oceans — first class with Air New Zealand, good food and good, steady speeds.'

We'd lost Simon in Auckland. When he'd signed on initially, he and his wife, Margaret had only one child, their little boy Benjamin. But Maggy gave birth to a second son just before the start and Simon's circumstances were altered drastically. He'd spoken to me before we left Cape Town to say that he would be getting off once *Lion* reached Auckland. We'd miss him but admired his commitment to his family. It would have been impossible for anyone else to have taken his place in a *Lion* group which, by that stage, was closer-knit than ever. So we made the decision to finish the race one man short. One thing was certain as a result of this: there would be more room in the ship's log without the repeated references to Si's sleeping habits.

I was determined that *Lion* would sail her own course in this leg, and not get sucked into a tactical situation with the other maxis. That's the way we did it with *Ceramco* and it worked well for her. It was all very well people saying we should stick with the opposition, but the truth of the matter was that the Farr boats, and maybe *Cote D'Or*, were quicker than *Lion* reaching, so it was no use following them. We didn't want to be taking any radical fliers, but we did need to do something different if we were to steal a march on them. Right now they seemed to be heading south at more of an angle than we were. I couldn't see any reason for that on the weather maps, so I was quite happy to let them go, while *Lion* did her own thing.

I'd also taken a punt and left most of our spare sails behind in Auckland. It might cost us if the main wardrobe didn't hang together. But we had a good sailmaking team on board for running repairs and the boat seemed to be going quite a bit faster without the extra weight. She was also steering better with the new rudder that had been built for us by Tim Gurr during the Auckland stop.

At about 0800 hours on Tuesday the 18th, less than three days out from the

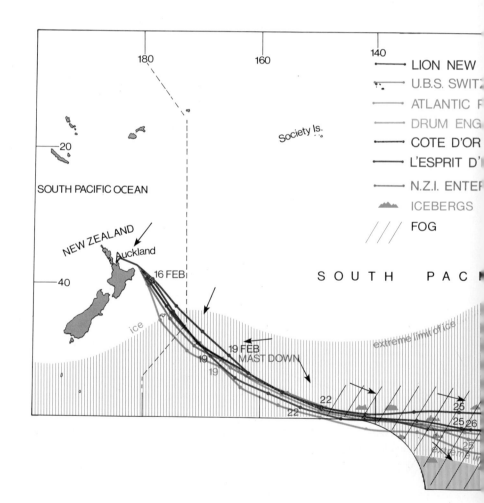

restart, *NZI*'s mast collapsed. She had been about 480 miles to the south-east of the Chatham Islands, making good time, close-hauled on port tack with 25 knots of breeze, when a diagonal supporting rod had broken. The mast folded, broken in two places — 50 feet above the deck and then again at the second spreaders. It took the *NZI* crew six hours to clear up the mess and retrieve everything before heading back to the Chatham Islands under jury rig. Although that meant one less boat for *Lion* to beat, and it was now between *UBS* and us for line honours around the world, we felt for the *NZI* crew, most of whom had become good friends, despite the supposed grudge between the two boats. Those of us who had been on *Ceramco* knew what they were going through.

NZI retraced her course to the Chathams, arriving there nearly three days later, during which time frantic efforts had been made to retrieve the remains of the original spar from Cape Town and bring it to Auckland. The plan was to marry the good parts of the two rigs, flying a team of experts to the Chathams to complete the work. But the plan failed and *NZI* was forced out of the race. I couldn't help but reflect on the mayhem caused among the maxis by the blow before Cape Town. If that blow

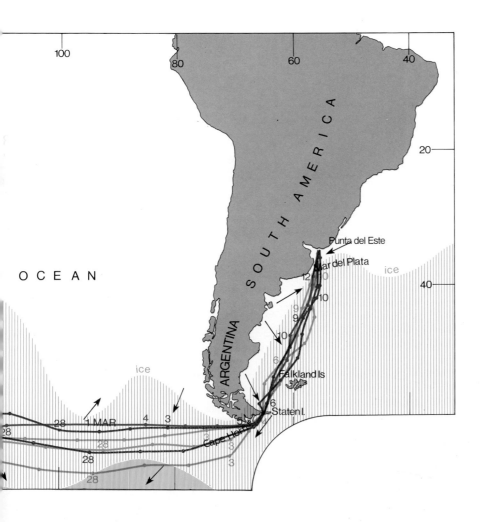

Beautiful sailing, Ed on the helm, off the New Zealand coast.

had occurred in the Bay of Biscay or at some other point further up the track, the maxi fleet would probably have been down to just two boats anyway — *UBS* and *Lion*.

We continued to head for our way-point in the middle of nowhere, holding slightly further north than the rest of the group, reaching quickly under either the NZ Line or the Air New Zealand kites. We'd been one and a half days ahead of *Ceramco*'s schedule as we went past the Chathams, so it had been a fast trip so far. During the night we overheard a radio exchange between *Atlantic Privateer* and *UBS*. Padda Kuttel asked: 'Pierre, the crew on board here want to know whether it will be this leg or the next — when your mast comes down, that is.' There was no response from the Swiss boat.

Later that day, after switching from spinnakers to big genoas as the wind came ahead, we sighted *Cote D'Or* on the opposite tack, crossing three miles behind our stern. On the radio sched we learned that *Drum* was 30 miles to the south-south-west of us, with *Atlantic Privateer* another 50 miles in the same direction. *UBS* was dead ahead, approximately 25 miles to the east-south-east. The log read: 'Now that we have left Real Kiwi Joker country, some questions remain unanswered: 1) Is Low Life really going to make an honest woman out of Robin (his girlfriend); 2) Is Shoeby really going to cash in his air ticket to NZ at the finish to buy one for South Africa; 3) Has Goddy really proposed to Fleur (reference to his girlfriend); and 4) Is it true that Combo is taking up pig farming after the race.'

Apart from a couple of short hitches, we'd been on port tack or gybe since leaving East Cape and life was becoming rather monotonous for the crew who didn't have a lot to do in the mild conditions. The luridness of the log entries increased apace with the boredom, particularly the entries by one crew member who shall remain

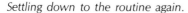
Settling down to the routine again.

Trucking again — with Goddy on the helm and Fuzz riding shotgun.

Anyone bring the rum and coke . . .

How would you like to run into that in the dark?

Do you remember that party . . .

anonymous but who weighed something in the region of 20 stone. A comment after one of his better (or worse) efforts predicted: 'The author of the above will end up with a little shop in Karangahape Road (Auckland's red-light district) selling adult books and marital aids, and spend his evenings as a barman in a strip club. He needs a psychiatrist.' But there were the wittier observations such as: 'Most people live on oxygen, Vonny lives on smoke,' a reference to Vonny's liking for cigarettes.

Lion was rattling along with runs consistently between 260 and 290 miles a day. We still sighted *Cote D'Or* occasionally and *Drum* wasn't too far away. But *UBS* had moved north of us while *Atlantic Privateer* seemed intent on collecting a few penguins. The sea and air temperatures were dropping and we were sailing through a lot of

Lion *digs her nose in and it's a case of going, going, gone with white water everywhere.*

murk, enough to make us turn the navigation lights on at night so that *Cote D'Or* and *Drum* would see us if they decided to alter course.

At 1615 hours when at 54 degrees 45 minutes South and 144 degrees 54 minutes West, we sighted a huge iceberg very close to starboard of us. It must have been at least 1500 feet long and 300 feet high with lots of bergy bits in the water around it, but mostly to leeward. The sea temperature had dropped to 4.7 degrees Celsius in the vicinity of this monster. I radioed its position to *Fazer Finland* which was following a similar track to us. We'd spoken to Micky Berner earlier in the day and he had reported less than 150 metres visibility.

In the next couple of days we sailed close to two more big fellas. They were an awesome sight, almost an iridescent blue with huge blue-green cracks or crevices marking the sides. We had to gybe to miss the second such berg, which was smack in our path, and about 10 minutes later we passed within about 15 feet of a big chunk that had obviously broken away from the main berg. We would need to be careful.

Just at that moment, the spinnaker halyard broke and the big Air New Zealand kite went down in front of the boat. I wasn't quick enough to bring the boat up into the wind, so we ran right over the top of it. By the time it emerged astern, it was tattered and torn where it had dragged under the keel, over the propeller and under the weed-guard on the rudder. The sailmaking team had quite a job on their hands and I was glad nobody from Air Lamb Chop was around to see what I'd done to the brand-new spinnaker which they'd bought us to replace the one we'd destroyed on that wild, rudderless run down the Northland coast to finish leg two. While the sailmakers got to work, someone wrote in the log: 'Peter Blake's scorecard — 1 rudder, 1 mainsail, 3 spinnakers, 1 genoa.'

Atlantic Privateer was now down as far as 58 degrees 30 minutes South while *Lion* was heading due east at 54 degrees 30 minutes South. We seemed to have lost a few miles to them, but *Lion* was trucking along at 16-17 knots so I couldn't see any cause for alarm. We were certainly jumping across longitudes at that rate and were now on a chart which had Cape Horn to the right-hand side of it. That was promising. We were only a week away and going like hell under heavy spinnaker and full main.

Feeling guilty about the Air New Zealand kite and the major job I'd created for the sailmakers — Trae, Shoeby and Fuzz — I asked them if they would like a small bottle of Long John whisky to keep them going while they were working up in the bow space. Fuzz replied: 'Yes thanks. Would you like some kahlua to keep you happy back there?' The 'thought for the day' in the log read: 'If man was supposed to sail

This leg is a lot colder, and Goddy retires accordingly.

around in these waters, why the hell did he build the Panama and Suez Canals?'

Late on the 25th, we learned that we'd been done by *Atlantic Privateer* and *Cote D'Or*, and even more so by *UBS*, although we'd put a few miles on *Drum*. We'd been averaging 14-15 knots but the boats further south had been averaging 15-16 knots. *UBS*, during this period on the way to the Horn, achieved speeds and runs which *Lion* had no hope of matching. Fehlmann later reported several 350-mile days. His best noon to noon effort was 352.9 miles, but his best 24-hour run was in fact an amazing 370 miles. That's an average of 15.5 knots for 24 hours and, by all accounts, *UBS* did it with little real fuss.

Lion meanwhile was becoming hard to steer while she averaged lower speeds and we were having the odd mild round-up, the boat tending to dig her bow under too readily for comfort. *L'Esprit D'Equipe* had radioed that she had damaged her mast below deck. But she was continuing towards Cape Horn under reduced sail while temporary repairs were affected. *L'Esprit D'Equipe* had suffered mast problems in leg two, so Dirk Nauta, on *Philips Innovator*, would be licking his lips. I wondered again what would happen to this fleet if the Southern Ocean really cut up rough, because so far it had been decidedly docile by previous standards.

But we had our own fright to remind us of where we were and how vulnerable everyone was. We were running hard in 35 knots of wind and decided to switch to a smaller kite at midnight. The heavy Hood chute was on two halyards, one of which jammed. With the skirt of the spinnaker flapping around on deck, the brace and the sheet unclipped themselves. There we were in near-gale conditions with a spinnaker streaming from the masthead on two halyards.

Ed went up in a special rigger's harness with the boat rolling all over the place. When he was halfway to the top the buckle on the harness came undone and he had to grab for the mast before he plummeted either to the deck or into the sea. Fortunately he was able to hang on, standing on the spreaders, until the crew could bring him down. Understandably shaken, Ed could not be sent aloft again, but someone had to go because the big red-and-white chute was still playing flags while *Lion* roared downwind at 15 knots under reefed mainsail only. Dalts didn't hesitate. Up he went to the masthead to tie a retrieval sheet to the spinnaker head before spiking the two halyards. The spinnaker floated down into the water astern and we had to stop *Lion* by bringing her up into the wind before we could get the kite aboard.

That lot was sorted out before we pulled the chicken chute up to resume our high-speed journey towards the Horn. That one lasted fully 10 minutes, the boat rocketing along and feeling good, until the halyard broke. We got the chicken chute aboard and considered the options, but with no spinnaker halyards left at the top of the mast, we had few. It would have been dangerous to send a man up with a new one. So we hoisted the No. 2 genoa and the jib top and carried on at reduced speed until, 10 hours later, we were in the position to go for a spinnaker again. The mishaps had cost us the best part of 30 miles, but we had to be relieved that we hadn't lost Ed. The log commented: 'Back to super flanker and full main and we're off once more after a rather trying night and morning, to say the least. Dalts did a marvellous job at the masthead and deserves a medal. We are lucky to have Ed still with us.' Then: 'Great work by Jaapi to replace external kite halyard.'

The Horn was now less than 1000 miles away — less than 1½ Hobarts — so we were cutting the Southern Ocean down to size. The days rolled by with the two remaining Farr boats — *UBS* and *Atlantic Privateer* — to the south of us and pulling

Bob repairs the jockey pole.

The riggers always had plenty to keep them busy.

slowly away. *Cote D'Or* was at last showing speed to match her length and she was doing similar runs to her Farr rivals. In these fresh conditions they were faster than *Lion* or *Drum*, reaching and running, and there was nothing we could do about it. We reconciled ourselves that from now on we would be racing *Drum* for second place on line honours. If, in the process, *UBS* hiccupped, that would be a bonus.

Our trials weren't over, however. We struck 36 hours of calms and light airs before our final approach to Cape Horn, and I was beginning to think that someone up there didn't like us. But the boats ahead finally began to falter. *UBS* was 36 hours in front of us when she reached the Horn and parked in light airs. *Atlantic Privateer*, coming up from her track well to the south of everyone, was encountering 20-knot headwinds. We'd taken 50 miles out of *Cote D'Or* and were pulling in *Drum* which reported light north-westers. The boys had been getting a Cape Horn strain of 'Channel Fever' as we closed in on the legendary landmark which was clearly going to be a highlight of the trip for those who hadn't been around before.

We were becalmed 40 miles to the west of the Horn early on March 5, and the rounding prospects didn't look good with so much black cloud and murk up ahead of us. But by the time we had the Horn abeam at 1025 hours, the sky had cleared and we went within a mile of the famous 'Cabo'. As we came abeam of the light, the Chilean navy contacted us on Channel 16. They have a permanent base in some huts on one of the eastern ridges of the Horn and we could clearly see the huge Chilean flag which they were flying. All they wanted to know was who we were, where we'd come from, how many people we had on board and where we were headed. Then they wished us a good day.

I asked them for a weather forecast and they replied 'calm', but I don't think they knew what they were talking about. Ever since then it had been freshening. The good news was that while we had been becalmed 40 miles to the west of the Horn, *Atlantic Privateer* and *Drum* had had similar problems in the Straits de le Maire between the south-eastern tip of Tierra del Fuego and Staten Island. *UBS* had taken off up the eastern coast of Argentina with a beautiful reaching breeze. But we were no longer concerned with her. We were keeping our attentions focussed on *Drum*.

There was little snow to be seen as we worked our way north-eastwards from the Cape along the coast of Tierra del Fuego, even though some of the closer mountains were between 3000 and 4000 feet and others further away were at least 8000 feet. But it was still a coastline of intrigue, the islands and bays looking most enticing, and I would love to go back there one day, with more time, and take a good look around.

But now we had the narrow Straits de le Maire ahead, and we were close-hauled in a very rough stretch of water with the night as black as pitch. My navigation had to be spot on — thank goodness for the satellite navigator — because there was a 4.5-knot current running with us, against the wind, which was kicking up such a nasty sea. But 4.5 knots under us was a big push and we shot through the channel like a cork coming out of a bottle. It was rough, with *Lion* crashing through big, steep, phosphorescent waves, but we were going like a rocket and things would have been a lot worse if that current had been against us as well as the wind. We put a lot of time on *Drum* in those 24 hours and now that we were beating in the same conditions as them, we would pile on the pressure. Coming through the Straits de le Maire was a bit disconcerting as I couldn't get a depth reading. There was nothing wrong with the equipment, so the water must have been too turbulent. This situation is not good for the nerves though. Now that we were clear of the straits, we had a constant 85-90 metres under us, but 'boy, was it boiling in the channel'.

Still hard on the wind to the west of the Falkland Islands, with 26 knots of breeze and a nasty short, steep sea, we were 93 miles behind *Drum*, 110 miles behind *Atlantic Privateer*, 160 miles behind *Cote D'Or* and 277 miles behind *UBS*. The smaller yachts had rounded the Horn and were reaching up astern in a north-westerly, *L'Esprit D'Equipe* still leading on handicap. But we couldn't do anything about them. *Drum* was our target. We had 1 day 18 hours on her when we left Auckland, so we had to finish within that time of her in Punta del Este, if we couldn't catch her before then.

BC, the bent cook who had done such a marvellous job so far, asked in the log: 'What am I doing here cooking for 20 mongrels, hard on the wind, pots leaping off the stove, when Simon Gundry, who got me into this in the first place, is down at the Masonic Hotel with all my mates laughing at me?' Someone replied: 'Never mind, BC, Gundry will miss the horror show in which we will be starring in a few days time. Look out Punta.'

In one 12-hour period on March 7 we took 30 miles out of *Atlantic Privateer*, 28 miles out of *Cote D'Or* and 15 miles out of *UBS*, but *Drum*, which had gone in closer to the Argentinian coast, was holding us now that we were out of the fresh upwind conditions and into lighter airs and flatter water. The on-deck crew were spending a lot of time on the weather rail with all of this windward work but they had a bonus attraction to keep them sane. Halley's Comet was perfectly visible when the frontal cloud cleared. We'd heard that hundreds of tourists, enticed to New Zealand to supposedly get the best view, were having problems seeing the comet, yet here we were getting a superb look at it. To celebrate, 'special' drinks were ordered from

Cape Horn in docile mood.

the galley and it was amazing just who had a small bottle of something stashed away in his bunk for a nip on a cold night. We'd heard from home that Raw Meat had appeared as 'Hunk of the Week' in one of the New Zealand tabloid weeklies. He was copping quite a lot of flak about his 'modelling career' as we entered the final stages of our journey to Punta.

By March 9 we had *Drum* 82 miles ahead, *Atlantic Privateer* 92 miles, *Cote D'Or* 118 miles and *UBS* 230 miles. We were still closing in on them and by the following morning we had cut the distance even further. But we were running out of time, and miles. The deck watch were still keeping an eye on Halley's Comet which, although no brighter than an ordinary star to the naked eye, was clearly visible through binoculars with a tail at least 10 times the diameter of the head. The consensus of opinion was that it was 'a) a UFO firing retros or b) a star with burnt-out rings'.

Late on the 10th we ran right out of wind, as if we were in the Doldrums again. The sea was glassy calm and what breeze there was boxed the compass. Over a six-hour period the log listed the wind direction as 303 degrees, 083 degrees, 320 degrees, 180 degrees, 245 degrees and 296 degrees. The observation alongside these entries said: 'Thick fog and f/all breeze. Food and water running low. Dalts going insane, armed guard placed on pantry. How much longer can we keep going?'

We waffled around until 0600 hours the following morning when Hughie at last decided to give us a break. From 1500 hours on the 10th to 0600 hours on the 11th we had covered only 52 miles, and at the worst of it we did one mile and then one and a half miles in successive hours. At 0800 hours we got word that *UBS* had 20 miles to go. The other three had put 60 miles on us during the night. Even worse, the smaller yachts had had a dream run up the Argentinian coast and *Philips Innovator*

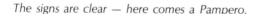

The signs are clear — here comes a Pampero.

was now only 60 miles astern. When it finally came, the breeze filled in with a bang — 30 knots from the west-south-west and we were off again, blast-reaching and averaging 11-12 knots. It backed to the south-west just before lunch and we changed up to the super-flanker and took off. The sun came out and suddenly everything, or nearly everything, was right with the world again.

The talk quickly turned to what the boys were going to do as soon as they hit port. On the daily radio sched I couldn't contact any of the other maxis and Meat said: 'Probably ashore mate, you can't get that many people in a telephone box.' His turn was not far away, however. He'd been caught hoarding lollies again and his punishment was to be tied up when we reached Punta and made to watch while we all ripped into a few cold beers.

We blasted along under the big Air New Zealand kite for the rest of the afternoon, the crew straining for every last ounce of speed for they could now almost smell that first beer. Then . . . crunch. We ran right out of wind again. Bloody hell, Hughie, what had we done to deserve that! Our only comfort was that we had a two-knot current under us and that at least was pushing us down the track in the right direction.

By 0400 hours on the 12th we'd picked up a light northerly. We were moving, but with 90 miles to go, dead upwind in that breeze. The log said: 'We're now picking on smaller targets than whales. Four-foot sunfish narrowly missed a large headache.' Then: 'Lion 1, Sunfish 0 — got one. Lion 2, Sunfish 0 — gotta nother one.' We waffled on until the northerly finally gained strength to allow decent progress and, at long last, made it to the finish-line off Punta del Este at 17.53.59 hours local time. *UBS* had finished 9 hours 19 minutes ahead of *Drum*, which had done a tremendous job over the final lap. She in turn was 1 hour 19 minutes ahead of *Atlantic Privateer*, with

It's late in the evening but there are plenty of people waiting to greet us.

Cote D'Or 18 minutes 14 seconds astern of her.

The calms had cost us dearly. *Lion* crossed the line 1 day 8 hours behind *UBS* and 23 hours behind *Drum*. This meant we still had 18 hours 7 minutes up our sleeve on our arch rival and near sister-ship for the final leg to Portsmouth.

LEG 3: AUCKLAND-PUNTA DEL ESTE

Elapsed Time	Days/H/M/S	**Corrected Time**	Days/H/M/S
1. UBS Switzerland	24.14.11.20	1. L'Esprit D'Equipe	22.07.54.53
2. Drum England	24.23.30.35	2. Equity And Law	22.17.42.47
3. Atlantic Privateer	25.00.50.25	3. Rucanor Tristar	22.22.33.21
4. Cote D'Or	25.01.09.11	4. Philips Innovator	23.01.10.20
5. Lion New Zealand	25.22.53.59	5. Fazer Finland	23.09.56.43
6. Philips Innovator	26.09.19.51	6. Fortuna Lights	24.06.10.21
7. Fazer Finland	26.12.15.43	7. UBS Switzerland	24.11.54.06
8. L'Esprit D'Equipe	27.00.50.39	8. Drum England	24.20.27.17
9. Norsk Data GB	27.15.45.41	9. Atlantic Privateer	24.21.00.54
10. Rucanor Tristar	27.21.05.10	10. Cote D'Or	24.23.37.51
11. Equity And Law	28.00.33.50	11. Lion New Zealand	25.17.31.32
12. Fortuna Lights	28.05.18.15	12. Shadow of Switzerland	25.17.58.04
13. Shadow of Switzerland	31.21.08.43	13. SAS Baia Viking	26.11.42.17
14. SAS Baia Viking	32.14.10.39	14. Norsk Data GB	27.04.28.50
15. NZI Enterprise	Did Not Finish	15. NZI Enterprise	Did Not Finish

Legs 1, 2 & 3

Elapsed Time	Days/H/M/S	**Corrected Time**	Days/H/M/S
1. UBS Switzerland	87.20.50.02	1. L'Esprit D'Equipe	83.08.49.28
2. Lion New Zealand	90.11.38.58	2. Philips Innovator	83.13.45.54
3. Cote D'Or	90.20.44.43	3. Fazer Finland	85.14.36.18
4. Drum England	91.05.46.02	4. UBS Switzerland	87.13.23.11
5. Philips Innovator	94.10.45.28	5. Rucanor Tristar	88.11.12.37
6. Fazer Finland	95.16.34.37	6. Fortuna Lights	89.14.25.13
7. L'Esprit D'Equipe	98.16.31.05	7. Lion New Zealand	89.18.09.06
8. Fortuna Lights	102.12.09.56	8. Cote D'Or	90.08.50.42
9. Norsk Data GB	103.06.58.23	9. Drum England	90.18.29.56
10. Rucanor Tristar	104.13.08.24	10. Equity And Law	93.08.24.45
11. Equity And Law	110.13.25.58	11. Shadow of Switzerland	96.17.44.36
12. Shadow of Switzerland	116.16.56.47	12. Norsk Data GB	101.18.14.36
13. SAS Baia Viking	129.02.04.23	13. SAS Baia Viking	109.05.09.52
14. Atlantic Privateer	DNF Leg 1	14. Atlantic Privateer	DNF Leg 1
15. NZI Enterprise	Retired	15. NZI Enterprise	Retired

NB: Cote D'Or incurred a 4 days, 1 hour, 56 minutes, 38 seconds penalty for fitting a new keel in Cape Town. This penalty is not included in the above tables.

9. Beat The Drum

It was now plainly evident that altering the start-time of the Whitbread race had changed the character of the race, and the feeling of having been cheated was only heightened by leg three. We'd had a maximum of three days of the hard, downwind running for which the race had become famous. If we hadn't sighted those icebergs and seen Cape Horn in daylight, it would have been difficult to believe that we had been in the Southern Ocean at all. Then there were the numerous calms. . .

My crew were asking, 'Who wrote the brochure?', and they weren't the only ones complaining. Padda Kuttel, bemoaning the fact that *Atlantic Privateer* had had to beat for eight days to reach the Horn from down south, when the chances of a north-easterly in those waters at that time of the year were only one percent, commented: 'The race is being held at the wrong time. It is too late in the year — the winds are too light and too fickle. The Whitbread should be about heavy-weather running, and lots of it.' *UBS Switzerland* hadn't broken anything, not even a halyard, and Pierre Fehlmann confessed that their hardest sailing had been between the Straits de le Maire and the finish in Punta del Este and that had been tactically hard as opposed to physically demanding.

I concurred with Kuttel's views. Heavy-weather sailing is part of the character of a round-the-world race. Boats and people should be put to the test, and this time they hadn't. My real concern, however, was that anyone considering the next race in 1989-90 might be lulled into a false sense of security by the events of 1985-86. The trend towards more lightly built hulls and lighter gear might lead to a Fastnet '79 situation, when a huge fleet of 303 boats had been caught in the Irish Sea by storm-force winds and freak seas. Fifteen people lost their lives, twenty-four of the boats that started were abandoned, five of them sank. Offshore racers had been getting frailer year by year in the quest to save weight. The result was the biggest disaster in the history of the sport.

The losses in that '79 Fastnet almost certainly would have been higher but for the fact that the fleet was caught out relatively close to land and within reach of assistance from a variety of sources. But what would happen if a similarly equipped Whitbread fleet got caught out in the Bay of Biscay or, God forbid, in the depths of the Southern Ocean, many thousands of miles from the nearest help? It was something the race organisers were going to have to consider carefully because the signs in the 1985-86 fleet were that some skippers had gone right to, or even past, the prudent limits in construction and gear.

The third leg had been a demoralising experience for the *Lion* crew but it was now that the unique camaraderie they had developed stood them in good stead. *Lion* was a distant fifth across the line in Punta, a full 32 hours 42 minutes behind *UBS* and only 10 hours 25 minutes ahead of the first of the smaller boats, *Philips Innovator*. That had nothing to do with sailing ability or boat speed. It was the luck of the draw as the weather played some diabolical games, with *Lion* mostly on the receiving end.

We were now 2 days 14 hours behind *UBS*. Line honours, barring some mishap to the Swiss yacht, were beyond us. But we still had 18 hours 7 minutes on *Drum*, which had sailed brilliantly to be second over the line in Punta. We would have one objective in the 6255-mile final leg from Punta del Este to Portsmouth — to beat *Drum*, or at least finish within 18 hours of her. That would make *Lion* second fastest around the world and there would be nothing wrong with that result.

The handicap situation was exclusively a battle of the smaller yachts. *L'Esprit D'Equipe*, despite her rig problems, had won the leg by 17 hours 15 minutes from *Philips Innovator*, and had regained the handicap lead overall. That lead was, however, only 4 hours 56 minutes, so the battle between those two to Portsmouth would be cut-throat. *L'Esprit D'Equipe* had trailed *Philips Innovator* by 12 hours 19 minutes leaving Auckland but had had a dream run across the Southern Ocean. She already had a strong hold on the handicap situation before rounding Cape Horn, then sped up the Argentinian coast without a pause, to clean up in a big way.

So, that would be the scenario up the Atlantic to England — *UBS* playing it conservatively with line honours as good as in the bag; *Lion* versus *Drum* for second fastest around the world; and *L'Esprit D'Equipe* versus *Philips Innovator* for the handicap prize.

Punta del Este is the Riviera of South America, a resort for the wealthy, and correspondingly exclusive and expensive in season. But the Whitbread fleet arrived

The **Lion** garden party was one of the hits of the Punta stay.

It's a BYO plant job.

When it comes to barbecues, those Uruguayans know their stuff.

at the season's close. We virtually had the place to ourselves. The restart was scheduled for April 9 so we had nearly a month to 'kill' in those pleasant surroundings before putting to sea again. With the season over, the accommodation was reasonably priced. We were housed in two-bedroom apartments which slept four and cost only $2000 a month, fully serviced.

The climate was similar to that of Auckland, the beaches were good, the people friendly and, with free membership of the superbly equipped Cantegril country club, we wanted for little. Some of the crews took off on sightseeing tours or shot home to Europe, but most people stayed close to Punta and relaxed. At the country club, we had full use of facilities which included a large swimming pool with diving boards, a full-size golf course, tennis courts, and horse riding. We had to get into the local habit of taking an afternoon siesta because the night-life, including restaurants, didn't start up until around 9.30 pm, but after a rigid watch system on *Lion,* this didn't pose a problem.

Pippa joined me in Punta, leaving Sarah-Jane with her grandparents in Emsworth, so it was a real holiday for both of us. The bachelors in the crew had a much tougher time seeking female companionship. In Mar del Plata, four years earlier, the *Ceramco* crew had claimed world records for 'holding hands' with the local ladies. In Punta, the *Lion* crew couldn't even claim that distinction. The social rules were so strict and the language barrier so difficult, they soon gave up the quest to concentrate on their golf or tennis. Once the Punta authorities and officials worked out what a round-the-world race fleet required when in port, most needs or requests were quickly satisfied,

Lion's shutter bugs prepare for photographic action as we head out to start leg four.

so it would be a good place for the fleet to return to in future races. But you could only go there out of the holiday season, that is, as the first or last stops in the race, otherwise it would be far too expensive.

I had one running problem while I was there. We had entered port without a Uruguayan courtesy flag. I should have had one on board but it had been forgotten in the press of other matters on my mind. Rear Admiral Charles Williams obtained a flag for us within two days of arriving·so we were correct in our etiquette. But the port authorities advised us that we had been fined US$300 and would not be allowed to leave Punta without paying the fine. I told them 'to take a running jump', they would have to send a gunboat out to prevent *Lion* leaving. Fortunately, there was no gunboat in sight as we went to the line for the start of leg four, only two elderly frigates which marked the start-line and which were otherwise occupied.

We had a new North mainsail which had been air-freighted to Punta from Auckland for the final leg. We'd tried it out a couple of days earlier and were delighted with the job that had been done by Tom Dodson and his team. Now, as we manoeuvred for the departure, *Lion* had so much more grunt in light airs than previously and was sailing higher and faster. I've no doubt that further attempts to make *Lion* as light as possible, even leaving some of the heavy-weather sails ashore, helped too.

I went for a conservative start with the 1.5oz kite and *Lion* trailed the rest of the maxis as we started to beat up the coast of Uruguay. But we were sailing higher and faster than everyone, with the possible exception of *UBS*, which we were at least matching, and morale was high as we set our sights on *Drum*, changing down to the No. 3 genoa, with full main, for a short-tacking duel close in to the shore.

We got through *Drum* fairly readily but stood too far offshore while she hugged

*The restart from Punta with **Fortuna Lights**, **Drum** and **Atlantic Privateer** down to leeward.*

the beach, so that the next time we crossed she was in front again. Lesson learnt — there must have been a fair amount of current running against us. So we stayed 150 metres from the surf. *Atlantic Privateer* came across to have a go at us. We sailed right through her lee and climbed out from under her bow — fantastic stuff! Kuttel didn't learn because he had another go when we crossed again. Same result, we climbed out from under him and spat *Atlantic Privateer* out the back. As night came we had *Cote D'Or* under control and had closed the gap on *UBS* to less than 400 metres.

So it went for the next three days, *Drum* always in close attendance, because there was no way we were going to let her stray, nor she us, and the other three in the vicinity and occasionally in sight, variously ahead or astern, to windward or leeward.

The crew had decided to spice up the last leg of their 'term' together by instituting a 'Dick of the Day' award. The first nominations were Vonny and Fuzz — Vonny 'for fighting Combo and breaking his hand', Fuzz because 'his engagement is on again'. Vonny won by a distance. I think my old mate, who was trying to give up smoking, yet again, was feeling a little irritable and, for once, the knife-edge repartee of the group had got on his nerves. He'd taken a half-hearted swipe at Combo and broken a bone in his hand in the process. There were no ill-feelings, however, and everyone quickly settled down to extracting the most from *Lion,* a new animal with that beautiful North main.

The first log entry for day four was: 'Drum very close now as dawn comes, about a mile to windward.' Then we picked up *Cote D'Or* as the breeze held at 8-10 knots from the south-east. Late the previous night we'd hit another whale, only a slight bump this time. It was quite noticeable that there were a lot more Jonahs this trip, so maybe the conservationists were winning their fight to save these giants of the oceans. Not that *Lion* was doing her bit on their behalf. The log recorded: 'Lion NZ (3 whales, 2 sunfish) 5, Whales and Sunfish (1 rudder) 1.' Someone suggested that we should stick little transfers on the bow as the fighter pilots in World War II did to record their 'kills'. But somebody else observed that maybe there were a couple of whales swimming around with *Lion* transfers on their heads.

The log also noted: 'Good conversation on deck today — on brain surgery, something we all know a lot about.' The 'Dick of the Day' award had gone to Dalts. Trae had run him a close second, for dropping his scrambled egg on the floor and only clearing up half of it before brushing the rest under the carpet (in this case a sail bag). But Dalts had a decided edge. When Shoeby had remarked that he (Dalts) looked a lot like *Kialoa* owner-skipper, Jim Kilroy, Dalts had retorted: 'Yeah, you're looking at a legend in the making.'

The wind had headed us until it was blowing from almost due north at a steady 18-20 knots. The radio sched the next morning informed us that *UBS* was 60 miles to the north-west of us but only 10 miles further down the track. *Norsk Data GB*, close in on the Brazilian coast, reported 50-knot winds and she had blown out her No. 5 headsail. With the wind increasing to 22 knots and the sea cutting up a bit, we ploughed on through the night with *Drum* always close to stern. We wondered whether it was going to be like this for the full 6255 miles. It was April 14, one year to the day since *Lion* left New Zealand on the delivery trip to Britain. That was 34,500 miles ago, yet it seemed like only yesterday.

It was very wet on deck with *Lion* close-hauled and tossing the water around. Jaapi won the 'Dick of the Day' award for managing to 'drown' his watch with one particularly good wave, but it was a close-run thing between himself, Goddy and Balls who had also excelled themselves in the same department. The log read: 'Drum still astern. Suggest we write to Mr Routing (as in Routeing Charts) to tell him that northerly winds do blow in this part of the ocean.' On the radio we heard that 28 'All Blacks' had gone to South Africa on an unofficial rugby tour. That would make the fur fly back home. The United States had bombed Libya. We wondered which event would get the biggest headlines in New Zealand.

Lion and *Drum* were now the most eastern of the maxis. *Cote D'Or* was 15 miles to the west of us and 15 miles further up the track. *UBS* was 45 miles to the west and 30 miles ahead, while *Atlantic Privateer*, seemingly intent on a flier, was 90 miles to the west of everyone and 15 miles astern of *Lion*.

The boat down below was beginning to smell a bit. There was too much water being chucked around to have the hatches open and the heat and humidity added to the problem. Some of the crew were also developing skin eruptions from wearing wet-weather gear over nothing else but shorts or underpants. But the breeze had begun to swing to the west and a squall brought 30 knots of wind and heavy rain. Oh, the relief! There was a scurry for shampoo and soap as everyone sought to take full advantage of a much-needed 'tub'.

Another note to 'Mr Routing' who said that the incidence of westerlies in this area was 'zero'. *Drum* had worked up on to our weather quarter but still couldn't get through. The sight of our stern must have been getting on their nerves by now. Her presence, however, was keeping the *Lion* team right on their toes. The breeze continued to swing, all the way into the south, and we were able to get a kite on

One of numerous sail changes off the Brazilian coast. Doldrums cloud ahead.

and open up the hatches to air the boat. The difference was immediate and greatly appreciated by the watch below.

We'd lost track of *Drum* during a rain squall and it wasn't until the following morning's radio sched that we learned she had grabbed the opportunity to break away. She was level with us, but 35 miles to the west. *Cote D'Or* was 11 miles directly ahead, while *UBS* was 53 miles in front of *Drum*.

We were still the best part of 1000 miles from the equator but the heavy downpours and wind swings had a feel of the Doldrums about them except that there was more breeze than one would expect in the Doldrums belt. Every downpour produced a rush for the toilet gear but few of them chose to wash over *Lion* and 'gunwhale bum', the dreaded lurgy of ocean-racing yachtsmen whose rear-ends spend too much time in damp or sticky surroundings, started to become a factor. The Doc's 'gunnel cream' became a popular little item.

Atlantic Privateer was continuing to slide off to the west and was maybe intent on finding something different to everyone else on the 'other side' of the Atlantic. But I could see no reason to change *Lion*'s direction. We were laying course up the Atlantic and making reasonable time, as the evening's position report confirmed. Only *Drum* had done slightly better than us, and we'd taken 31 miles out of *UBS*. *Cote D'Or*'s position had us confused. The plot said she was 30 miles to the east of us but we had her in sight, only eight miles to the east of *Lion*. This demonstrated that the Argos system wasn't perfect.

If we were looking for Doldrums conditions, and we weren't, we found them the next day. The wind became fitful, in strength and direction, and progress slowed with lots of rain clouds all around. It was weird. We'd sit there struggling in a light breeze, while there was flat water 100 metres away to leeward, but white horses 200 metres away to windward. The downpours had diminished to become constant drizzle. Not to be denied their 'tub' to relieve the heat and humidity, the crew had discovered a 'bath' in the foot of the mainsail which was an immensely effective water catcher. By sitting with your rear-end over the drain hole in the sail, you could have quite an effective 'bath' in the fold that was created in the foot of the sail by the flattening reef. And it was amazing what a good wash would do to morale.

Right then our spirits needed lifting too. We were enjoying a tremendous match race with the other maxis, but the little boats were killing us, bringing up more wind from astern while we were waffling in mostly light headwinds. The morning sched on April 18 had all the maxis within 22 miles of one another (*Atlantic Privateer* had rejoined the fray), while the smaller yachts, led by *Philips Innovator* and *L'Esprit D'Equipe*, were only 15 miles astern.

During one of our spells of flat calm, Glen went over the side to take some photographs under the boat. Fuzz went down, too, to check the keel and the propeller gear. Unaware of this Ralph used the toilet and flushed it at the precise moment that Glen was close to the outlet, for which Ralph was a favourite for the 'Dick of the Day' award. Ralph also took first prize in the daily scrabble school, of which the log observed: 'It appears that a good vocabulary is not a criterion for success at scrabble.'

Finally, we found out why the smaller yachts had closed right in on us. A front had moved in from astern bringing 30 knots of breeze and heavy rain. We were off and running with the 1.5oz spinnaker. The breeze was a touch beyond the red-and-white kite's range, so we peeled to the Air New Zealand spinnaker, as the rain moved through to leave us with a beautifully sunny day and southerlies of 10-20 knots. We

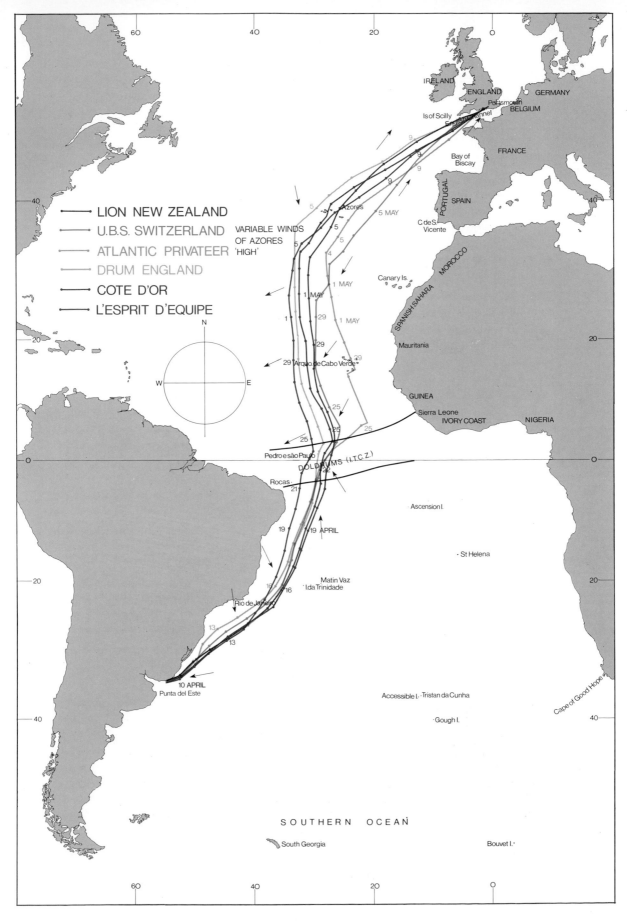

LEG 4 PUNTA DEL ESTE-PORTSMOUTH

changed back to the 1.5oz and settled down for some real sailing. We were two days away from being abeam of Recife, in Brazil, which is on the most eastern tip of South America, and 4093 miles from Portsmouth.

The evening radio sched was unbelievable. *Fazer Finland* and *Philips Innovator* were actually ahead of us on the water, if well to the west and closer to the Brazilian coast. *L'Esprit D'Equipe* was just three miles astern and even the veteran *Norsk Data GB* was only 20 miles astern in terms of distance to go to the finish. What should have been a 6000-mile race was now just 4000 miles in which we had to save our time on handicap.

Shoeby was found fast asleep on watch that night, stretched out on the No. 2 headsail which was on deck, ready if needed. The log commented: 'Reckoned he was checking stars, but it took five minutes to wake him with methods that included sounding the fog horn, booting him in the head, poking him in the ribs, and whispering his Jaapi girlfriend's name in his ear.'

On we waffled, sometimes thinking we were in the south-east trades, but then grinding almost to a halt as the breeze played tricks. The crew was working flat out with the sail changes and we were still managing highly respectable 240-mile days. But they were hard miles.

It was April 21. We'd been at sea for 13 days, and there, ahead, lay what had to be the Doldrums. A simply massive cloud stretched across the horizon in front of us. As we approached, the cloud seemed to swallow up all of the wind, then everything went haywire and we were lashed by torrential rain as the crew ran through the sail changes — 1.5oz kite to staysail, staysail to windseeker, windseeker to staysail, staysail to windseeker, windseeker to No. 1 medium genoa — in eight knots from the north-north-west. Welcome to the Intertropical Convergence Zone! *UBS* had talked with a ship heading south in our area that reported little wind from 3 degrees North to 3 degrees South. The prospects weren't good.

That night, we heard that *UBS* had done a number on everyone. She and *Atlantic Privateer* had been within sight of each other approaching a cloud formation. *UBS* had got to the cloud first and disappeared. When *Atlantic Privateer* got there, she parked. But *UBS* had obviously kept going in her own private breeze. She was now 30 miles ahead and going away, still with breeze. Those Swiss either had an extraordinarily fast boat or they were exceptionally lucky, or a bit of both. *Lion*'s log observed: '1200 hours, one hell of a big, black bastard is coming over.' Then: 'The

A bloke could swim faster . . .

Fuzz takes the opportunity to check out the propeller gear.

158

big, black bastard comest and verily soakest the bastards on deckest.' We were at 3 degrees 47 minutes South, 28 degrees 40 minutes West.

Several times over the next six days we thought we were through the Doldrums belt only to get caught up again in the light, fickle airs and calms that used to be the dread of the old sailing-ship days. As day merged into monotonous day, Balls didn't endear himself to anyone when he revealed that he was reading James A. Michener's *The Covenant* which recorded one voyage from England to Cape Town taking 209 days.

Two days into the windless belt, Ralph was unlucky enough to get a finger caught between the genoa car and the back-stop on the track. The pulp of flesh was sliced off to the bone, so the Doc was called on to perform his first 'operation' of the trip. He cleaned and dressed the decapitated digit but there wasn't much more he could do. It would take several weeks for the flesh to granulate back. In the meantime, the Doc would change the dressings every day and check for any signs of infection. The Doc certainly got himself involved in some weird and wonderful dissertations as the on-deck watch whiled away the frustrating hours. One evening I heard him teaching Fuzz all about taking out appendixes and gall bladders while, in return, Fuzz was teaching the Doc about sails.

BC went about his business as usual, doing a superb job in the galley and seldom even bothering to stick his head up. He had everything absolutely organised in the galley department and kept churning out meals that were nutritious and imaginative considering the limited resources at his disposal. Every day he could be found baking another batch of four loaves — two for lunch and two for breakfast the following morning. His scones were an eagerly anticipated treat.

The only consolation during this near hiatus in the racing was that everyone else, figuratively speaking, was in the same boat — *UBS* being the exception. She had paused only briefly and by the 24th was 145 miles to the north and 80 miles to the east of us. *Atlantic Privateer* looked to be getting clear too, but was continuing east while *UBS* was headed north. Both reported 10-knot easterlies. The weather map showed that the Azores High, the next hurdle we would have to overcome, was relatively weak and a long way north of its usual position, hence the 'creeping Doldrums' which were shifting north with us to keep the bulk of the fleet in their clutches. I couldn't see any reason to begin formulating tactics for the high as yet. We would keep making best speed north until we escaped the Doldrums, and then

Into the trades again and time for a clean-up.

The Ed Danby school of splicing — Andy the pupil.

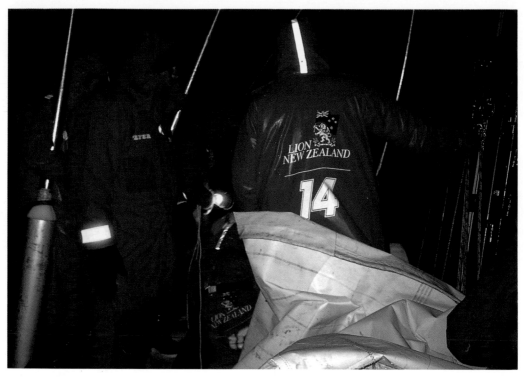
Quick repairs to the windseeker, on deck in the middle of the night.

we would tackle the Azores.

We finally emerged late on the 26th. There had been promising indications that we were through during the previous 16 hours with the breeze firming enough to get our hopes up. Then, at 2000 hours, the wind increased to 19-22 knots from the north-north-east and we were off again with full main and No. 4 genoa. There were a number of occupational therapy' schools in progress by this stage. Ed was teaching Raw Meat about wire-to-rope splicing, the Doc taking an interest too. Trae was running a gymnasium and Whale was going to a 'finishing school'. Everyone had agreed it was time that he tidied up his act, particularly since we would be going ashore permanently in a couple of weeks. It was a tough assignment, however. The log noted: 'Roy not willing to join Whale's school of clean speech as it would mean him learning a whole new language.' Roy had distinguished himself earlier in the leg by managing three uses of the 'magical F word' in a four-word sentence.

Atlantic Privateer, with Kuttel complaining that people weren't giving their positions on the daily sched, had gone silent on us, but the Argos plot showed that she was 400 miles to the east of the main group. She'd continued on port tack, heading for Africa, after emerging from the Doldrums, but now was on starboard heading north. Kuttel was obviously trying to slip through to the east of the Azores High but to me the risks in that were great. *UBS* was 250 miles ahead of *Drum, Lion* and *Cote D'Or,* which were in a line from west to east — *Drum* furthest west and a little further north than *Lion, Cote D'Or* to the east and about level with us. By the next day we would be at the same latitude as the Cape Verde Islands, for which *Atlantic Privateer* was

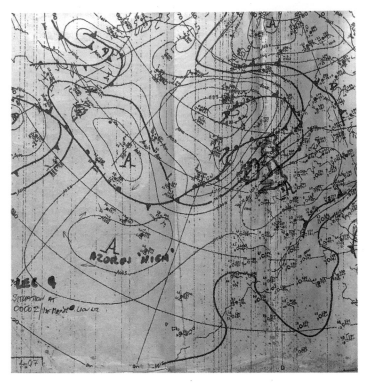

The Azores High was to the west of its usual position but then wandered slowly east with the fleet.

headed, and probably five or six days from the Azores.

The weather maps became increasingly interesting as we closed on the Azores Islands. The Azores High was now centred dead in front of us with a low to the north-east of it and two smaller systems forming on the eastern seaboard of the United States. The forecast was for the Azores High to intensify and move east into the Bay of Biscay, trailing an oblong tail. With luck we would have the two low pressure systems, to the west and north, to provide a nice funnel of wind to take us around the back of the high and speed us to Britain.

The Argos report now showed that *Atlantic Privateer* was 450 miles to the east of us, in among the Cape Verde Islands and making extremely slow progress. *UBS* was 225 miles to the north and 115 miles east of *Lion,* while *Drum* was 54 miles north and 75 miles west. It appeared that *UBS* was covering the boats on both sides of the Atlantic, while *Drum* was driving off in a bid to get north as quickly as possible. *Cote D'Or* was 33 miles south and 90 miles east of us.

There wasn't going to be an easy passage around the Azores High. It remained almost stationary and intensified to 1040 millibars. By 1900 hours on May 2 we were parked in flat calm water and a maximum one knot of wind. The log observed: 'Flat as Twiggy's tits.' The only good news of the day, as far as I was concerned anyway, came from Pippa. She reported she was pregnant, and that was good enough for a celebratory rum all round.

The log asked: 'Why does our skipper smile today?' I'm afraid the drink was a bit too much for Balls, who was on galley duty and doing an excellent job, until

Spinnaker change coming up, the Azores astern.

he sampled the temporarily unaccustomed liquor. Balls snuck a couple more and had to retire to his bunk. He was a natural for the 'Dick of the Day' award, but for some reason was unable to make it to the prizegiving ceremony to collect his trophy.

On May 3 nobody bothered to record *Lion*'s daily run. It was less than 100 miles, and we managed only 103 miles to noon on May 4. There were now numerous references to Twiggy's anatomy in the log and I doubt that the lady would have been flattered by them, no matter how accurate they were in terms of the weather and the sea which had us trapped. To make matters worse, we heard on the radio that the rebel 'All Blacks' had gone down 24-19 in the first 'test' in South Africa. Jaapi was socially ostracised.

The smaller boats, which had again come chomping up behind the maxis, were now feeling the effects of the calm and slowing down. The only boat which wasn't affected was *UBS*. She'd snuck around to the east of the high and picked up winds off a low that had been stationary to the west of Ireland, but which now was shooting away, taking *UBS* with it. There was absolutely nothing we could do about her, and we had enough to keep us occupied with *Drum* which was further north and west than us and so in a better position to pick up wind first if the Azores High refused to move on. We were 1500 miles from the Lizard, at the south-western tip of England, and still 360 miles from the Azores themselves.

Finally, late on the evening of May 4, we picked up a breeze again. It was only 8-10 knots from the west-south-west, but that was a veritable gale after what we'd been through. As we picked up speed through incredibly smooth seas, a trans-Atlantic jet passed overhead and the log recorded: 'Kerosene canary slipped by at 400 knots, its contents sipping cocktails and watching a movie. Makes one wonder!' That started a deep cockpit discussion on what would we do if a jumbo jet came down intact alongside us. Where would we put the 350 survivors? Mac D got the 'Dick' award. He'd fallen asleep on deck, wrapped up in the No. 1 light genoa, and hadn't woken up until the sail was on its way up the mast when . . . exit one startled Mac D.

May 5, and *UBS* was spearing away towards Britain's Western Approaches. She was 410 miles east and 90 miles north of *Lion*, a massive 375 miles closer to the finish. Fehlmann disclosed that *UBS* had slowed for only a matter of hours before picking up a developing north-westerly, which had gradually freed to send the Swiss powering away under spinnaker while the rest of us were sitting becalmed. *Cote D'Or* had emerged from the calm 48 miles closer to the finish than *Lion* and was 85 miles to the east of us, while *Drum* was the same distance ahead of *Lion* but 30 miles west and 120 miles north.

I'd called New Zealand through Portishead Radio the previous night, speaking to Craig Armstrong and Vaughan Dennison at the Homai School for the Blind. We chatted for about eight minutes on a good line, the two lads clearly excited by talking to *Lion* so many miles away in the middle of the Atlantic. At the completion of the conversation, Portishead came back on and said: 'No charge for that one.' A nice touch.

The breeze wasn't quite settled in direction, swinging from the west to the east, and then back again to the south-south-west, but it at least kept blowing at 7-15 knots. Going through the Azores we got a beautiful view of the lights of Terceira off to starboard. We reached off so that we weren't affected too much by the shadow of its 3347-foot mass, then hardened up again to pass through the channel between Terceira and Sao Jorge. The smell of land was strong — the first land we'd seen in 27 days, and it prompted a virulent strain of 'Channel Fever' among the crew.

Vonny was involved in a porridge fight and had to spend the rest of the morning cleaning up the mess, and Meat was caught red-handed with another cache of hoarded lollies. Where did he get them all? But there was caution too. We'd been trapped by light airs so often in this race nobody was prepared to believe that we were really on our way to the finish. The log said: 'Channel Fever starting to appear.' Then: 'Channel Fever disappearing with another bout of light air.' And then again: 'The breeze seems to have left us again, very unusual, that. Combo just about to slit his wrists.' There followed an opinion on the heritage of the New Zealand yachtsman's wind god which read: 'Hughie is a malicious, cantankerous, conniving, cunning, malevolent bastard — but he certainly is a funny sod.'

This really was it, however. The breeze built again that night and by the following afternoon the log was saying: 'Good old Hughie (he says hopefully), going like a rocket.' The barometer was dropping slowly to support the new-found optimism, and the fleet sched revealed that we'd scored by sailing through the Azores instead of around them. *Drum*, *Lion*, *Cote D'Or* and *Atlantic Privateer* now formed a line across the ocean at right angles to the course to the English Channel — *Drum* to the west, then *Lion*, *Cote D'Or* to the east of us, and *Atlantic Privateer* coming in from the cold to try and salvage something from Kuttel's punt on going well to the east.

The wind backed through to the south, then to the west and built to 35 knots — almost the most breeze of the trip. We went up from the NZ Line kite to the Air New Zealand spinnaker, the super-flanker, and then the heavy runner as we took off for a spot of welcome 'Rambo stuff'.

It looked like *UBS* was going to comfortably beat *Flyer*'s Round the World race record of 120 days 6 hours, with 96 hours in which to do 680 miles. But we weren't going to beat the 1981-82 time, the calms had seen to that, even though we were now averaging better than 13 knots with surfs to 17 knots in a strong and steady southerly. It was going to be close for second place between *Drum*, ourselves, and *Cote D'Or*. *Drum* was 10-15 miles closer to the finish. We had the same distance to run as *Cote D'Or* and 40 miles less than *Atlantic Privateer*, which didn't have as much wind astern of us.

UBS had averaged 14 knots for the last 12 hours and had 500 miles still to go. But it was going to be another small-boat bonanza on handicap. *Fazer Finland* was only 70 miles astern of us, while *L'Esprit D'Equipe* and *Philips Innovator* were only about a day behind.

Another close encounter with a whale prompted the log entry: 'Lion just about mounted Aran. High-speed sailing is great fun.' By noon on the 8th we had 760 miles to go to the Needles at the western entrance to the Solent. The wind had moderated to around 20 knots, but it was still south-westerly and we were cracking on the pace. Now in a position to get a little cheeky, someone wrote in the log: 'The health department is going to close Cole's Dirty Dick restaurant down in three days. Shit hot. Rolling off easy miles dead on course. Cold fog on deck. Raw Meat gives the regular scrabble school a lesson in the finer points of the game, which again goes to show you don't need a good vocabulary, or in fact any vocabulary at all, to win at scrabble.'

We had gear problems in the night, the masthead U-bolt on the spinnaker halyard exploding and necessitating an 'all hands' call, and then a spinnaker pole-end failure which cost more time. We still averaged 11 knots for five hours, but *Drum* and *Cote D'Or* had found better breeze to the north of us and were looking dangerous. *Drum* had 60 miles on us and, with the south-westerly showing signs of abating, that might be enough to nobble us for second fastest around the world.

There was relief ahead, however. The breeze stayed at 20-24 knots and was forecast to, if anything, increase. It went more to the west in the next 24 hours, but the forecasters were right, as it increased slightly in strength and we roared through the Western Approaches and into the English Channel. We couldn't catch *Drum* and *Cote D'Or* but we had our time on our arch rival and she wouldn't escape now. We also had *Atlantic Privateer* sewn up, 60 miles astern.

We listened to the F.A. Cup final between Liverpool and Everton as we chased up the Channel, knowing our old mate Seffo would be glued to the television in Portsmouth, loving every minute of Liverpool's 3-1 win. The only thing we envied him was the celebration party afterwards, but our own celebration was now less than 20 hours away. The final entry in the log was: 'Frustration upon frustration as orgasmic surfing waves go by (wind against tide), but not enough breeze to catch them.'

We were on our way in through the Needles Channel with only 12 miles to run. It was a grey and bitterly cold Sunday morning but who gave a damn. There was the ferry with all of our wives, families, relatives and friends aboard, and even the old J-class *Valsheda* came close to have a look as we swiftly closed on Gilkicker Point, still running hard under the Air New Zealand kite. One last sail change, kite down and No. 4 genoa up, and one final, short board upwind to the finish-line off the entrance to Portsmouth Harbour. We crossed at 1053 hours GMT. *Drum* had beaten us in by 5 hours 44 minutes, but overall we had still beaten her by 12 hours 22 minutes to be second fastest around the world. On this occasion, that was no mean effort.

Blasting up the Solent with only a few miles to go.

*The J-class **Valsheda** comes out to greet us.*

The line crossed, Southsea in the background. Been there, done that.

LEG 4: PUNTA DEL ESTE-PORTSMOUTH

Elapsed Time	Days/H/M/S	Corrected Time	Days/H/M/S
1. UBS Switzerland	29.17.41.40	1. L'Esprit D'Equipe	28.14.20.19
2. Cote D'Or	31.09.46.12	2. Philips Innovator	29.07.45.42
3. Drum England	31.13.08.29	3. Fazer Finland	29.10.12.52
4. Lion New Zealand	31.18.53.00	4. UBS Switzerland	29.15.23.52
5. Atlantic Privateer	32.01.55.49	5. Rucanor Tristar	29.22.16.34
6. Fazer Finland	32.12.50.24	6. Equity And Law	29.22.18.59
7. Philips Innovator	32.16.15.12	7. Cote D'Or	31.08.14.29
8. L'Esprit D'Equipe	33.07.44.14	8. Fortuna Lights	31.09.41.22
9. Norsk Data GB	34.18.17.13	9. Drum England	31.10.04.25
10. Rucanor Tristar	34.21.17.57	10. Lion New Zealand	31.13.29.13
11. Equity And Law	35.05.41.40	11. Shadow of Switzerland	31.18.10.42
12. Fortuna Lights	35.09.13.00	12. Atlantic Privateer	31.22.05.21
13. Shadow of Switzerland	37.21.58.03	13. Norsk Data GB	34.06.57.34
14. SAS Baia Viking	41.16.49.06	14. SAS Baia Viking	35.13.44.13
15. NZI Enterprise	Did Not Start	15. NZI Enterprise	Did Not Start

Final Details

Elapsed Time	Days/H/M/S	Corrected Time	Days/H/M/S
1. UBS Switzerland	117.14.31.42	1. L'Esprit D'Equipe	111.23.09.49
2. Lion New Zealand	122.06.31.58	2. Philips Innovator	112.21.31.37
3. Drum England	122.18.54.31	3. Fazer Finland	115.00.49.10
4. Cote D'Or	126.08.24.33	4. UBS Switzerland	117.04.47.03
5. Philips Innovator	127.03.00.40	5. Rucanor Tristar	118.09.29.12
6. Fazer Finland	128.05.25.01	6. Fortuna Lights	120.19.06.37
7. L'Esprit D'Equipe	132.00.15.19	7. Lion New Zealand	121.07.38.18
8. Fortuna Lights	135.21.22.56	8. Drum England	122.06.19.29
9. Norsk Data GB	138.01.15.36	9. Equity And Law	123.06.43.44
10. Rucanor Tristar	139.10.26.21	10. Cote D'Or	125.19.01.50
11. Equity And Law	145.19.07.38	11. Shadow of Switzerland	128.11.55.19
12. Shadow of Switzerland	154.14.54.50	12. Norsk Data GB	136.01.12.10
13. SAS Baia Viking	170.18.53.29	13. SAS Baia Viking	144.18.54.05
14. Atlantic Privateer	DNF Leg 1	14. Atlantic Privateer	DNF Leg 1
15. NZI Enterprise	Retired	15. NZI Enterprise	Retired

NB: Cote D'Or's time includes a penalty for a keel change in Cape Town.

UBS — went like a Swiss watch.

Never more, Sailor
Shalt thou be
Tossed on the wind-ridden
Restless sea.
Walter De La Mare
Never More Sailor

10. I Did It My Way, But . . .

UBS Switzerland had the Camper & Nicholson marina at Gosport to herself for one and a half days after she crossed the finish-line. The fractional rig Farr 80-footer, so well campaigned by the experienced and totalitarian Pierre Fehlmann, was first home from Punta del Este by 1 day 16 hours. She had gone around the world in 117 days 14 hours 31 minutes 42 seconds, breaking *Flyer's* 1981-82 record by 2 days 16 hours 2 minutes 32 seconds. What might her time have been had the weather been more conducive to fast sailing?

Lion New Zealand was fourth across the finish-line in Portsmouth, trailing *UBS* by 2 days 1 hour. *Cote D'Or* had beaten us in by 9 hours 6 minutes, and *Drum England* had pipped us by 5 hours 44 minutes. But our much-maligned Holland 78-footer was still second fastest around the world in a time of 122 days 6 hours 31 minutes 58 seconds. *UBS* had beaten us by 4 days 16 hours, and we were 1 day 23 minutes outside *Flyer's* time.

The big boats were annihilated on corrected time, the Briand 57-footer *L'Esprit D'Equipe,* skippered by Lionel Pean, more than 5 days 5 hours ahead of the first maxi *UBS*. *L'Esprit D'Equipe* encountered mast problems again in the fresh conditions in the Western Approaches. That made it three legs out of four in which her spar had threatened her chances. But she hung together long enough to beat her arch rival *Philips Innovator* by 22 hours 21 minutes on handicap, picking up 17 hours of that in the final leg. *Philips Innovator* was second on corrected time, the stock racer-cruiser *Fazer Finland* third and *UBS* fourth. *Lion* finished 9 days 8 hours behind *L'Esprit D'Equipe* on handicap, seventh in the final analysis.

Britain had distinguished itself by almost ignoring the race finish. If Simon Le Bon, plus his partners Paul and Mike Berrow, had not been aboard *Drum* for the second half of the race, the 1985-86 Whitbread would have come and gone with the British media hardly aware of its happening. As *Lion* completed the final miles up the Solent, she was escorted by Rear Admiral Charles Williams, the race director, in the official reception launch, our own supporters' ferry and a couple of photographers' runabouts. The J-class *Valsheda* had closed in for a look but she was on her way out sailing, anyway. We couldn't complain because it had been the same for Fehlmann and his crew as they completed their record-breaking run. But we couldn't help compare the scene with that in Auckland when the maxis arrived and, more particularly, with the reception *SAS Baia Viking* had received, 16 days off the pace and dead donkey last. It made one wonder whether the event was starting and finishing at the right venue.

There was no time to be too reflective, however. The *Lion* boys were in port, they'd completed what they'd set out to do nearly 20 months earlier, they were surrounded by relatives and friends, and there were dozens of cold, hard-earned Steinlagers to be consumed. There were Pippa and Sarah-Jane, one taking a very protective interest in her daddy, the other slightly disappointed that because of her condition she couldn't really join in the party with her usual gusto. And there too were Pippa's folks, Judy and John Glanville, plus her sister, Louise and brother, Charles. Tom Clark, Alan Topham, John Balgarnie, Mark van Praagh . . . it seemed that everyone who had been instrumental in bringing the project to fruition was on deck to see the race completed.

The crew was in top form, as closely knit now, probably more so, as when they set out on the campaign, and they were extremely good fun to be around. The realisation that shortly they were splitting up and going their own ways made some of the toasts and speeches a little sad, but it was touching to see people who had been 'Rambo'-type characters for the best part of 20 months let the veil slip and reveal that beneath the hard exteriors there were attractively soft centres. I watched them go through their 'after-match' repertoire. They were a great crew, had committed themselves to a major undertaking, and each in his own way contributed to *Lion*'s success.

Dalts: At times he over-drove the boat to advantage, at others he pushed *Lion* beyond the limits. At first I didn't think he quite appreciated the time or the point at which we had to reduce sail, which is important in a race like the Whitbread. But he could not be faulted in his enthusiasm for the job he had to do. Nor could one question his courage. The time he went to the masthead in the middle of the night, spending some time up there in a full gale, with the boat jumping all over the place, to spike the jammed halyards, was something I wouldn't have liked to do. Yet Dalts took it all in his stride.

Mike: A natural leader who didn't have to work at getting the best out of people. Always pleasant, he got on well with everyone and worked extremely hard at his watch-keeping duties. If there was anything else to do about the boat, he would be involved, particularly on the sailmaking side of the project. In port, he was in charge of the sails, making sure that everything was repaired and maintained, taking a big weight off my shoulders. He'd been promoted to watch leader when Ross Guiniven got off after the Hobart race and had proved an inspired choice.

Doc: Perhaps one of the quietest people on the crew, he had done a moderate amount of ocean sailing before joining *Lion,* but benefitted greatly from the delivery trip to England. His professionalism in the medical department was greatly reassuring to me and I was sure that if we had had any major problems he would have dealt with them. Initially he suffered from seasickness but got over some of this problem when we changed the keel on *Lion* and the motion improved. He was always conscientious and I couldn't have asked for anyone better in his place.

Simon: When he first joined the project, Si was all enthusiasm. But a second child had come along earlier than anticipated and this naturally altered his view of life. He felt a little uneasy, even guilty, at leaving his wife, Maggie, at home with two little boys, aged less than 18 months. I could understand this, appreciated his concern and did not put anything in his way when, in Cape Town, he told me that he would, provided I agreed, be leaving the boat after leg two. He was missed for he was particularly good at organising the crew ashore and was a strong, experienced hand on board. Some people felt he got off in Auckland because *Lion* wasn't performing as well as we might have expected. I knew this to be untrue and I admired his concern for his family who, after all, were far more important than any Whitbread race.

Fuzz: He came on board feeling he was a very good trimmer. By the time we'd finished the race, he *was* a very good trimmer. Fuzz was a highly amusing character who, for some reason, was the butt of a lot of fairly pointed humour. But he was quite capable of handling it all, and of dishing out his fair share too. He was an extremely hard worker and good to have on board.

Shoeby: The race hadn't altered Kevin. He was the same good-natured character who had embarked on the programme 20 months earlier. It had improved him though, and what he had learned about seamanship and trimming would stand him in good stead for the next item on his agenda — trying out for the New Zealand 12-Metre team in Fremantle.

Trae: A genuinely nice guy who excelled at virtually everything he did, from trimming to public relations. If anything, his delightfully dry sense of humour became even more acute as the race progressed. Another member of the sailmaking team, Trae was one of the strongest people on board. A deep thinker, he would do anything to make the boat go faster and never had a down moment.

Mac D: Paul was one of the easiest-going characters on the boat. He was always smiling, a favourite with the ladies wherever we went and absolutely conscientious about everything to do with the campaign. One of the engineers — the complicated winch and steering systems were his responsibility. I never had to worry, all the right spares were always to hand along with the expertise to put things right.

Bob: Mac D's offsider in the engineering department and similarly expert and conscientious. Bob was also one of the best bow men I'd come across and was invaluable on the delivery trip as a watch leader. He and Mac D had done a lot of sailing together and came highly recommended by Martin Foster. They both lived up to Martin's confidence, and then some.

Ralph: He took quite a lot of getting to know as he was one of the quiet types on board. Fit and strong, he proved to be one of our best heavy-airs helmsmen and knew what he was doing when conditions got tough, as they did going towards Cape Town. He always did what was expected of him and made a very valuable contribution to the project.

Roy: He suffered from a back problem which was a little more serious than I realised and which affected his agility around the boat. But he was absolutely invaluable in other areas as he knew the constructional and installation details of *Lion* inside out and could, and would, tackle any job. Fairly quiet at sea, he didn't make a fuss about much and was a good sea-mate to have along. I was pleased he was part of the crew.

Balls: One of the quietest members of the crew, Graeme took some getting to know. He proved an excellent seaman, reliable at his job around the deck. He would always be in the thick of things and had no qualms about conditions, no matter what the weather or how tough it was.

Glen: I raised a few eyebrows when I picked him because Glen didn't fit the image of a rough and tough round-the-world yachtsman. He surprised them all and for me was probably the 'find' of the trip. He was the best helmsman on the boat, in all conditions, and made up for any lack of strength on the helm when it was rough with sheer skill and concentration. He also fitted in well, no matter what the crew was up to, and did everything that the others attempted, often bettering them. Outgoing and personable, he was a tremendous ambassador for the boat and for New Zealand.

Goddy: With Glen, he was the 'find' of the campaign. Goddy hides his light under a bushel much of the time but has talents and attributes which made him a real strength in the crew. Apart from being a very humorous person, he steered well, trimmed well, worked well about the boat and was one of those New Zealanders who can happily turn their hand to virtually everything.

Whale: The harder it got, the better Aran liked it. A big lad in every sense of the word, we never saw him with his spirits down, or without a bag full of dirty books. When things got bad, he'd be up there calling the shots from the sidedeck while Dalts steered, controlling the boat. One of the few guys who had the sheer strength to haul the wheel-lock to lock even when the boat was doing 25 knots.

Cole: BC got a good introduction to long-distance sailing on the delivery trip. A person with a very even temperament, he never got ruffled and was another with a deceptive sense of humour. He probably spent more time in his bunk than anyone else aboard, but that was probably because he was so efficient at his job in the galley. In 30 minutes, he could produce breakfast for 22 people and everyone would be happy. If we put someone else in there, which we did now and then to give Cole a break, it would take them three times as long to do the same job, they'd make ten times as much mess and use five times as much food.

Jaapi: He was good for the project from start to finish. His knowledge of big boats was a real asset and he was an expert rigger who enjoyed what he did. To watch him and Ed at the top of the mast, 100 feet above the deck, working away for several hours to feed through a new halyard in a big seaway, was quite something. Jaapi would steer occasionally but didn't want to take control of the scene. He was happy being good at what he was doing in another area of responsibility, and I thoroughly appreciated that.

Ed: He was one of the great personalities on board. He knew all about long campaigns having done two British challenges for the America's Cup. With Bob, he was one of the best bow men I'd experienced, among the best in the world. Those two lived at the end of the spinnaker poles or, in Ed's case, up the mast. An expert rigger, he and Jaapi probably spent more money in their department of the boat than anyone else, but only to ensure that *Lion* was always in full racing trim.

Guy: Combo came on board late, when the crew was already into its stride as a special entity. Yet he was accepted, and fitted in readily. A very strong person, the harder the work the better he liked it. He was also a good seaman who liked to work out what was going on and how it could be improved. He was always down below helping to repack sails and proved a genuine asset ashore with his ability to talk to people about all sorts of subjects.

Vonny: He hadn't changed in the slightest since the 1981-82 race on *Ceramco*. Vonny enjoyed being on deck this time, as opposed to being in the galley, and was usually quiet but enthusiastic. He enjoyed the race for different reasons to the others and was the one guy in the crew who could always be found chatting to crews of the other yachts, genuinely into international relations.

Meat: Andy completed my trio of 'finds' for this campaign. Extremely strong, he wanted to help with everything, even to being on deck during the other watch because he thought he might help the boat to go faster. To begin with he was somewhat overawed by the experience of some of the people he was sailing with but he soon overcame that. He was the butt of a never-ending stream of jokes and spent an inordinate amount of time tied up to the rigging. But that was because the other guys liked and enjoyed him so much. He was one of our best helmsmen, grinders, mastmen, tailers, sail-baggers — you name it.

I had no doubts they were the best crew in the race and was only sad that the boat we'd sailed wasn't quite as highly capable. Deep down, and as a group, we'd accepted this a long time before. We'd had our suspicions during the pre-race build-up in Britain. Those suspicions had been confirmed in leg two when we found there was nothing we could do to keep *Lion* up with the Farr boats when they took off downwind in the fresher stuff. But *Lion* was the boat we had, and *Lion* was the boat we would sail to the maximum. We would push her as hard as possible and then see if the rest could sustain the same sort of pressure. The outcome might have been different had the conditions been more Whitbread-normal, but they weren't — and that was yacht racing.

In this race in milder conditions, Pierre Fehlmann and *UBS Switzerland* had proved unbeatable. Good on them! But I couldn't help feeling a little disappointed with the Ron Holland design office, even though the ultimate responsibility for *Lion New Zealand* was mine. We'd gone to them for the ultimate Whitbread maxi, a boat which would be as light as the Farr boats turned out, but a lot stiffer with a lot more sail.

Lion wasn't that boat, even though the Holland office assured us they could achieve the design features and figures we specified. Instead of being 31 tons actual weight, she was close to 38 tons. The keel was about right and so was the rig, so nearly all of that extra weight was in the hull, deck, the internal stiffening bulkheads and space frame and fittings, which meant that the hull and deck were approximately 50 to 60 percent overweight. The boat, I knew, had been built precisely to designer specifications and we had been extra careful with the weight and positioning of

KZ-5

LION NEW ZEALAND

Lion — *right boat for the wrong race?*

everything that went into or onto the yacht. Yet *Lion* ended up floating five inches below her original lines. It takes a lot of weight to push a maxi that far down into the water. The result was a yacht which, all-up, was 20 percent heavier than what we were seeking, with a righting moment which was the lowest of the maxis, when we had set out to achieve the highest. To cap it all, the rating came in at 67.4ft IOR instead of the maximum 70ft IOR. We were handing the opposition performance and handling advantages even before we started, and all we had to offset this was a boat which, we were understandably sure, wouldn't break.

Still, *Lion* had been, and remained, a good yacht — as she had proved in the last leg going up the Atlantic and there were times, particularly in the blow going to Cape Town, when we had been thankful for her constructional integrity. In some ways she was the right boat for the wrong race. Or maybe it was the wrong race for the right boat. Whatever the case, crew and boat had given it their best shot, and in the process had been tremendous ambassadors for New Zealand.

On this occasion, second fastest around the world had to be good enough. But next time. . .

Appendices

1985-1986

1985-86 WHITBREAD ROUND THE WORLD RACE AWARDS

Trophy	Awarded For	Winner
Whitbread Trophy	First on corrected time	*L'Esprit D'Equipe*
R.N. Club & Royal Albert Yacht Club	Second on corrected time	*Philips Innovator*
Royal Thames Yacht Club 'Valsheda' Trophy	Third on corrected time	*Fazer Finland*
Long John Trophy	First on elapsed time	*UBS Switzerland*
Henri Lloyd Trophy	Second on elapsed time	*Lion New Zealand*
Portsmouth City Council Trophy	First in Division A	*UBS Switzerland*
R.N.S.A. Decanter	Second in Division A	*Lion New Zealand*
First in Division C	Corrected time	*L'Esprit D'Equipe*
Second in Division C	Corrected time	*Philips Innovator*
First in Division D	Corrected time	*Rucanor Tristar*
Second in Division D	Corrected time	*Equity And Law*
Roaring Forties Trophy	First on corrected time (legs 2 and 3)	*Philips Innovator*
Best Production Yacht	Corrected time	*Fazer Finland*
Best Maintained Yacht		*UBS Switzerland*
First Woman on Handicap		Ann Lippen, *Rucanor Tristar*
Most Outstanding Personality		Gustaaf Versluys, *Rucanor Tristar*
Most Outstanding Seamanship		Skip Novak, *Drum*
Excellence in Communications		Peter Blake, *Lion*

Previous Whitbread Race Results

1973-74 WHITBREAD ROUND THE WORLD RACE
Course: Portsmouth — Cape Town — Sydney — Rio de Janeiro — Portsmouth

	Rating	Elapsed Time Days/Hrs/Min/Sec	Corrected Time Days/Hrs/Min/Sec
1. Sayula II	42.4 ft	152.09.11.08	133.12.32.43
2. Adventure	40.2 ft	162.19.06.30	135.08.03.45
3. Grand Louis	43.4 ft	162.01.19.41	138.14.52.06
4. Kriter	50.6 ft	156.14.10.03	141.01.53.35
5. Guia	34.9 ft	177.19.23.48	142.19.20.40
6. Great Britain II	69.0 ft	144.10.43.44	144.10.43.44
7. Second Life	55.6 ft	161.02.02.47	150.08.06.19
8. CS & RB	37.1 ft	187.00.21.46	155.06.57.06
9. British Soldier	43.8 ft	179.19.49.53	156.20.53.19
10. Tauranga	39.1 ft	185.20.42.52	156.22.23.43
11. Capernicus	33.0 ft	204.19.48.50	166.19.01.22
12. 33 Export	44.2 ft	197.10.02.24	174.22.28.22
13. Otago	41.7 ft	203.21.31.14	178.08.49.10
14. Peter Von Danzig	42.1 ft	204.15.30.55	179.14.50.40

1977-78 WHITBREAD ROUND THE WORLD RACE
Course: Portsmouth — Cape Town — Auckland — Rio de Janeiro — Portsmouth

	Rating	Elapsed Time Days/Hrs/Min/Sec	Corrected Time Days/Hrs/Min/Sec
1. Flyer	48.4 ft	136.05.28.47	119.01.00.00
2. Kings Legend	48.4 ft	138.15.47.23	121.11.17.23
3. Traite de Rome	35.7 ft	154.20.58.12	121.18.50.59
4. Disque D'Or	46.2 ft	142.00.37.48	122.10.56.23
5. ADC Accutrac	46.9 ft	145.15.28.11	126.20.18.36
6. Gauloises II	38.1 ft	156.23.00.36	127.07.54.35
7. Adventure	37.5 ft	158.14.12.35	128.02.54.28
7. Neptune	44.3 ft	152.05.33.35	130.11.52.48
8. B&B Italia	41.5 ft	157.05.34.48	132.02.22.47
9. 33 Export	39.7 ft	164.15.31.47	133.00.31.11
10. Tielsa	50.0 ft	148.13.22.11	133.00.36.00
11. Great Britian II	68.4 ft	134.12.22.47	134.10.43.11
12. Debenhams	41.3 ft	161.05.05.23	135.19.49.48
13. Japy Hermes	45.1 ft	164.01.29.23	143.06.00.00
15. Heath's Condor	68.8 ft	143.01.41.59	144.00.09.35

1981-82 WHITBREAD ROUND THE WORLD RACE
Course: Portsmouth — Cape Town — Auckland — Mar del Plata — Portsmouth

	Rating	Elapsed Time Days/Hrs/Min/Sec	Corrected Time Days/Hrs/Min/Sec
1. Flyer	67.8 ft	120.06.34.14	119.01.12.48
2. Charles Heidsieck	54.6 ft	131.21.34.35	120.07.55.29
3. Kriter IX	52.1 ft	134.07.37.42	120.10.50.26
4. Disque D'Or	46.0 ft	143.13.00.28	123.11.45.17
5. Outward Bound	40.0 ft	151.15.19.30	124.11.55.03
6. Xargo III	44.4 ft	147.15.10.18	124.19.02.37
7. Morbihan	37.2 ft	156.12.34.17	125.15.24.45
8. Berge Viking	42.4 ft	149.20.57.51	125.16.54.17
9. Alaska Eagle	50.4 ft	142.04.56.52	126.10.51.44
10. Euromarche	60.8 ft	134.15.28.42	126.23.37.40
11. Ceramco New Zealand	62.9 ft	132.11.55.38	127.17.42.43
12. Skopbank of Finland	38.0 ft	158.09.54.32	128.15.06.47
13. Rollygo	39.6 ft	157.12.41.33	129.20.52.12
14. Traite de Rome	34.6 ft	166.10.40.09	130.23.58.41
15. Croky	33.7 ft	170.00.22.24	133.23.34.43
16. FCF Challenger	69.6 ft	138.15.27.12	138.15.27.12
17. United Friendly	68.0 ft	143.22.23.50	141.10.06.55
18. Walross	36.8 ft	177.07.16.44	143.19.36.03
19. Licor 43	51.4 ft	174.14.59.02	160.02.16.35
20. Ilgagomma	40.0 ft	187.12.47.22	160.09.22.55

N.Z. International Yacht Racing Trust Committee

Admiral Sir Gordon Tait (patron)
Sir Thomas Clark (chairman)
Alan Topham, OBE (publicity and sponsor liaison)
John Balgarnie (finance)
Michael Clark (fundraising)
Jock O'Connor (public relations)
Mark van Praagh (public relations)
Sylvia Dunbar (secretarial)
Ross Laidlaw (secretary to Trust)
Peter Blake, MBE (skipper and project manager)
Tim Gurr (boatbuilder)

Trustees

Banks Peninsula Cruising Club
Bay of Islands Yacht Club
Bluff Yacht Club
Bucklands Beach Yacht Club
Canterbury Yacht and Power Boat Club
Devonport Yacht Club
Invercargill Yacht Club
Lake Taupo Yacht Club
Mangonui County Yacht Club
Nelson Yacht Club
New Plymouth Yacht Club
Panmure Yacht and Boating Club
Ponsonby Cruising Club
Royal Akarana Yacht Club
Royal New Zealand Yacht Squadron
Royal Port Nicholson Yacht Club
Tauranga Yacht and Power Boat Club

Main Sponsors of *Lion New Zealand*

Lion Breweries Ltd
Air New Zealand
Atlas Corporation Ltd
Auckland Coin and Bullion Exchange Ltd
Chase Corporation Ltd
Construction Machinery Ltd
Fay, Richwhite & Co. Ltd
Healing Industries Ltd
John Andrew Ford
McConnell Dowell Corporation Ltd
Mogal Corporation Ltd
New Zealand Line
Newmans Group

Trade Suppliers and Project Supporters

Aerospeed Services NZ Ltd: customs agents
Alliance Freezing Co. (Southland) Ltd: freeze-dried meats, fish, yoghurt, vegetables, fruit
Don Alexander Sound Systems: P.A. systems at various functions
Alan Anderson: meat supply in England and NZ, sponsor liaison
ANZ Banking Group (NZ) Ltd
Apex Machinery Ltd: general heavy-grade tools
Auckland Harbour Board: Harry Julian, Bob Lorimer and Capt. Ross Blair (harbourmaster), captain and crew of *Hikinui* (floating crane)
Auckland Milk Corporation: fresh milk
Auckland Milk Products Ltd
Bad Bins Ltd: disposal of builders' rubbish
Alister Ball: fund-raising badges
Bowring Burgess Marsh & McLennan: insurance
B.P. New Zealand Ltd: fuel for cars, heating, *Lion*'s motor
Carlton Cranes Ltd: all lifting work
Caxton Paper Mills Ltd: printing paper, toilet rolls, paper towels
CED Distributors Ltd (Apple): computer equipment
Cookes Consolidated Services Ltd: wire rope
Dickinson's Metal Foundries Ltd: keel bolts and propeller shaft
Diners Club NZ Ltd: major promotion assistance
Dorlon Products Ltd: wet-weather gear, safety equipment, foam for bunks, material for bunk covers, flooring
Dunlop Slazenger NZ Ltd: all sleeping bags
Feltex Ropes: synthetic ropes
Flexible Hoses Ltd: all pipes, hoses, hydraulic lines, exhausts
Foodtown Ltd: enormous quantity of food
A. Foster & Co. Ltd: general chandlery
Fox & Gunn Ltd: balsa core material
Graham Products: design and development of rig fittings
Hood Sailmakers NZ Ltd: sail inventory
Hurley & Williams Ltd
Institute of Sport Health: crew fitness
Lane Walker Rudkin Group (Canterbury): all crew and project clothing
R.A. Lister NZ Ltd: main engine (Gardner) and generator (Poranha)
Lucas Industries NZ Ltd: lead acid batteries; pouring of 16-ton lead keel
Kenneth Lusty Ltd: electrical installation, supply of sailing instruments and electrical equipment
Mathias Meats NZ Ltd: freeze-dried meats, Zodiac dinghy, Evinrude outboard; sponsor liaison
Metropolitan Life Group: radio spots support on RNZ
Mitsubishi NZ Ltd: four 6-man liferafts
Morris Black & Matheson Ltd: Makita tools and general tools
Penfolds Wines NZ Ltd: wine supply
Radio New Zealand: all communications equipment
Radmore Marketing Associates Ltd: sponsor liaison
Rutherford Marine Ltd: raft servicing; sponsor liaison
Shorters Car Sales Ltd: courtesy car
Southern Communications Ltd: radio and communications equipment
South Pacific Credit Card Ltd (Amex): major promotion assistance
APV Technicast Foundries Ltd: specialist metal foundry
UEB Industries Ltd: cartons
Vision Optical Co. Ltd: Bolle sunglasses and snow goggles
The Wood Yard Ltd: timber for the plug
Yachtspars NZ Ltd: spars and rig

Dept of Trade and Industry
NZ Apple and Pear Marketing Board
NZ Dairy Board: powdered milk and cheeses
NZ High Commission, London
NZ Hydrographic Dept: all charts and admiralty publications

NZ Meat Board
NZ Produce Markets: fresh fruit and vegetables
NZ Spit Roast Co.: launching day food
NZ Wines and Spirits Ltd
NZ Wools Board: warm clothing
Willis Faber Johnson and Higgins: insurance
Citizen Watches: waterproof watches and clocks
Docksider Shoes (Andrew Donovan): boots and shoes
Scania Trucks: Zodiac dinghy assistance
Sanyo: washer/drier for delivery trip
Hansen and Berry: fund-raising badges
Towers, London: meat supply
Greg Scott Agencies: upholstery and covers
Vicks: cough medicine, project support
Orewa Pharmaceuticals (Peter Rig): full medical kit
Philips: stereo and video equipment
Dataform Press: computer paper
Waitaki NZR: meat supply
The Mad Butcher: BBQ meats and equipment
Guzzini: glasses and crockery
Repco: lottery promotion assistance
TNT Alltrans: freight assistance
H.L. White Carriers: general carriers
Russell Plant: pontoon
Hutchwilco: flare demonstrations
Harrison Marine: Evinrude outboard motor

Ron Holland Yacht Design office
Bruce Woods and Bret de Thier: interior design and coordination
Peter Montgomery: radio reports; personal support
Alan Sefton: journalist reports; personal support
John Toon: project film-maker

Gisborne Harbour Board
Lyttelton Harbour Board
Napier Harbour Board
Nelson Harbour Board
New Plymouth Harbour Board
Northland Harbour Board
Otago Harbour Board
Picton Harbour Board
Southland Harbour Board
Tauranga Harbour Board
Timaru Harbour Board
Wellington Harbour Board

Captain's Club Members

1. Mr & Mrs E.G. Engel
2. Bob McMillan,
   McMillan Motors Ltd
3. Marsden Alexander
   Motors Ltd
4. Michael Clark,
   Michael Clark Ltd
5. Mr W.R. Bryce,
   Michael Clark Ltd
6. Mr L. Hawke,
   South Auckland
   Caravan Centre
7. Mr J. O'Connor,
   David Brett Ltd
8. D'Arcy MacManus
   & Masius Ltd
9. Bruce Martin,
   Kirk Motors
10. Mr & Mrs G.C. Leitch
11. Mr L.R. Allen
12. Mr V.J. Allen
13. Cancelled
14. Mr T.R. Burton,
    Trevrex Equipment Ltd
15. Mr & Mrs J. Tannahill
16. Mr & Mrs W. Allan
17. Mr B.E. Marshall
18. Peter Cornes,
    Godolphin Laing Ltd
19. The Electric Construction
    Co. of NZ Ltd
20. Mr E. Lloyd Sibun
21. Mr R.J. Allsopp-Smith,
    Millar Samson Ltd
22. Mr G.A.F. Bendall,
    Devonport Yacht Club
23. Bruce C. Westbrooke,
    F.E. Westbrooke & Son
24. Stephen B. Fisher,
    Fisher International Ltd
25. Mr R.D. Dee
26. Mr J.N. Thomson
27. Ray Haydon,
    Ray Haydon Ltd
28. R.D. Slater & P.C. Leitch,
    Rodpet Enterprises
29. Keith Wendell,
    Wendell Real Estate Ltd
30. Mr W.S. Romanes,
    Venture Treks Ltd
31. Bob Sinclair,
    Apex Machinery Ltd
32. Mr T.B.N. McNeill,
    Danish Mineral
    Research Ltd
33. Stan Bonsel,
    C.H. Bonsel Ltd
34. Trans Pacific Marine Ltd
35. Mr G.A. Davies,
    D. & W. Motors Ltd
36. Mr B.R. Winstone

37. R.W. & J.M. Scherer,
    Dominion Containers Ltd
38. Mr W.B. Jackson,
    Jackson Stead & Co Ltd
39. Baron Ralph von Kohorn
40. Mac Convery,
    Shiguchi Woodcraft
41. Alan Lennane,
    TGA Yacht & Power
    Boat Club Syndicate
42. Capt. G.W. Dunsford
43. Mr R.F. Wilson
44. Mr J.H. McDowell
45. Mr W.J. Ratcliffe,
    Bumper Service Ltd
46. Mrs J. Gibbs,
    Gibbs Securities Ltd
47. Mr T.M. McCall
48. Mr E.A. Goodwin,
    Anderson Goodwin Ltd
49. Mr M.B. Sheffield
50. Mr T.L. Marusich,
    Dalma International Ltd
51. Mr J. Wood,
    Woolyarns Ltd
52. Mr K.M.P. Smith,
    Ceramco Ltd
53. Mr G.W. Blithe
54. John & Glenda Neil
55. Allan McPhee,
    Lion Breweries Ltd
56. Royal Akarana Yacht
    Club Inc.
57. Mr C.J. Kerr,
    B.P. Oil New Zealand Ltd
58. Peter W. Fitzsimmons,
    Metropolitan Life
    Assurance Company of
    N.Z. Ltd
59. Mr F.G. Snedden
60. Mr D.R. Levene,
    Levene & Co. Ltd
61. Torr family,
    Torr Holdings Ltd
62. Mr T.G. Tobin,
    Glenfield Auto
    Services Ltd
63. Keith R. Gerrie,
    GTE New Zealand Ltd
64. Mr H.R.H. Paul
65. Mr H.E. Buchanan,
    Buchanan's Chemists &
    Druggists Ltd
66. Fred Bailey,
    Fred Bailey Eng. Ltd
67. Mr & Mrs H.H. and
    J. Blampied
68. Mr N.G. Ritchie
69. Mr D.J. Weatherhead,
    Diners Club (NZ) Ltd

70. John McC. Webber,
    N.Z. Glass
    Manufacturers Co.
71. Mr J.B. Hay
72. Mr G. Coombs,
    Australian Balsa Co.
    Pty Ltd
73. Mr D.A. Garrett,
    Garrett's Catering
    Services Ltd
74. Mr D.I. Harrow,
    Willis Faber Johnson
    & Higgins
75. William McCullough
    Hogg Robinson (NZ) Ltd
76. Craig A. Barnes,
    Dream Merchant
    Waterbeds Ltd
77. Bruce Taylor,
    Commodore Computer
    (NZ) Ltd
78. Mrs S.E. Hines,
    Jim Hines Interior
    Services
79. Mr K.J. Tobin,
    Glenfield Motor Centre
80. Gavin Walter,
    Gloucester Wool Baa Ltd
81. Barry Jeffery,
    Jeffery Enterprises Ltd
82. Mr W.F. Titchener,
    Conform Plastics Ltd
83. Mr R.J. Percy
84. John A. Steer
85. Mr W.M. Kember,
    Produce Markets Ltd
86. Bryson Richards,
    Braemar Motors Ltd
87. Mr L. Belz,
    Trigon Plastics Ltd
88. Mr & Mrs B. Blake
89. Graeme Russell
90. Mr I.N. Amoore
91. Mr C.P. Wickham,
    Det Norske Veritas
92. Messrs Bruce, Rodney &
    Anthony Ewing,
    Ewing Boating Services
93. Mr J.D. Musin,
    American International
    Underwriters (NZ) Ltd
94. Bob Ferri,
    Avis Rent A Car
95. Mr W.S.L. Stichbury
96. Mr A.A. Martensen
97. Mr M.H. Hughes,
    Concrete Cutting (NZ) Ltd
98. Graham Shaw,
    G.K. Shaw Ltd
99. Mr M.J. Mulcahy,
    Mulcahy Engineering Ltd

100. Mr L. Cramer,
Excalibur Marketing
International Ltd
101. Mr D.J. Hall,
The Hall Manufacturing
Co. Ltd
102. Cameron J. Shaw,
G.K. Shaw Ltd
103. Mr A.G. Hughson,
Mason King & Partners
104. A. Del J. Johnston,
Nat. Mutual Life Assn
105. Mr A.W.L. Yaxley,
Packaging House Ltd
106. Mr G.R. Land,
Stephenson & Turner
107. Rear Admiral L.G. Carr
108. Paul M. Carter,
Carter's Photo Service Ltd
109. Mr K.R. Waters,
Classic Waterbeds Ltd
110. Mr H.R. Baker,
Tainui Press Ltd
111. Mr J.N. Stephenson,
Fisher Stoves (NZ) Ltd
112. B.G. Morrison,
Concord Joinery Ltd
113. Mr R. Onnes
114. Mr R.F. Bratt,
Emoleum — Neuchatel
115. Dr N.A. Algar
116. Mr S.J. Ellis,
Ellis Industrial
Consultants NZ Ltd
117. Mr E.V. Henry,
Fletcher Fishing Ltd
118. Mr & Mrs J. Mutch
119. Mr D.J. Bransgrove,
Hibiscus Motel
120. Mr M.K. Coe,
Amalgamated Wireless
Australasia
121. Mr P.A. Harris,
NZ Enamelled
Products Ltd
122. Mr W.B.C. Evans,
Dunlop NZ Ltd
123. Mr J.B. Harding,
Scenic Tours NZ Ltd
124. Mr J.R. Wheadon,
Sincerity Dry Cleaning
Co. Ltd
125. Mr L.E. Moylan
126. Mr B.L. Hurrell
127. Mr R. McCapra,
Coates Brothers (NZ) Ltd
128. Mr J.R. MacKay,
Jaymac Transport Ltd
129. Mr E. Joy
Building Services
(Engineering) Ltd
130. Mr B.W. Yarnton,
J.S. Yarnton Ltd

131. Mr E.J. Skill,
Crane Accessories Ltd
132. Mr M.W. O'Donnell
133. Mr J.C. Clapp,
Atlantic & Pacific Travel
International Ltd
134. Mr J.C. Clapp,
Atlantic & Pacific Travel
International Ltd
135. Mr B.R. Perry,
Brian Perry Holdings Ltd
136. Mr R.M. Sherson,
Sherson Construction Ltd
137. Mr B. Smith,
Bruce Smith Ltd
138. Mr & Mrs D. McNiel
139. Marcel Fachler
140. Mr D.R. Mosley
141. Mr T.M. Perry,
Raven Yachts
142. T. Perry & V. Mischefski
143. Warren H. Conway,
Port Craig Timber Co. Ltd
144. Mr R.A. Patterson,
Gibco New Zealand Ltd
145. Mr G.M. Philp,
Victory Autos Ltd
146. Mr E.W. Farrell,
Metal Spinners Ltd
147. Mr A.N. Lawson,
Southern Photography
148. Mr D.L. Hook
149. Mr R.P. Thesiger,
Gearbulk Shipping
NZ Ltd
150. Scott Yates,
Associated Personnel
Consultants Ltd
151. Mr H. Small,
Healtheries of NZ Ltd
152. Mrs A.D. Gibbons
153. Graham Guy,
Guy Engineering Ltd
154. Mr R. Savory,
R. Savory Ltd
155. Mr M.D. Domett,
Domett Transport
Holdings Ltd
156. Mr F.J. Prichard,
Dealer Systems Ltd
157. Mr J. Vryenhoek,
Matons Enterprises
158. Mr W.J. Weinberg,
Weinberg Wools Ltd
159. Peter Hojsgaard
160. Mr W.G. Dunster,
Fabric Bindings Ltd
161. Mr J.A. McLeod,
Waikato Times Ltd
162. Rick Woodroffe,
Woodroffe Advtg Ltd
163. Mr B. Alston,
Fox & Gunn Ltd

164. Mr J.D. Harper,
Johnson Wax NZ Ltd
165. Barry Briggs,
Safe R Brakes Ltd
166. Staff of G.W. Dunsford
& Associates Ltd
167. Gavin Wright
168. Rob Maxwell,
Presco Piston Ring
Co. Ltd
169. Bob Playle,
Ven-Lu-Ree Ltd
170. J. & K. Davern,
James Davern Ltd
171. New Plymouth Yacht Club
172. Puflett & Smith Ltd
173. Mr & Mrs R.J. Finlayson
174. Steven Finlayson
175. Catherine Finlayson
176. Sylvia Dunbar
177. Barry McKenzie,
Topline Nurseries Ltd
178. Mr R.T. Wallis
179. Gerhard Ammermann,
Bayer NZ Ltd
180. Mr D.M. Ross,
William Cooke
Holdings Ltd
181. Mr G.D. Wills,
Konsun Lau NZ Ltd
182. Lon Higgins
183. Mr J.R. Snell
184. Mr R.C. Morris,
Regency Stainless Ltd
185. Mr Colin J. White,
Coronet Peak Ski Area
186. Angela M.C. Bowron
187. Mr F.W. Little
188. Jon W. Skinner,
Byron Shelley Ltd
189. UEB Industries Ltd,
Packaging Division
190. Mr A.R. Griffin,
Auckland Coin & Bullion
Exchange Co. Ltd
191. David Cook
192. Eagle Marketing
Services Ltd.
193. David Keruse,
Keruse & Gairdner Ltd
194. Gary Forman,
Forman Insulation Ltd
195. Skellerup Industries Ltd
196. Mr C.R. Forbes,
Forbes Enterprises Ltd
197. Mr M.L. Griffiths
198. J.D. Edmonds,
'Pride of Auckland'
Cruise Co.
199. Don Thomson,
Hood & Thomson
Motors Ltd

200. Mr D. Littlejohn,
     NZ Line
201. Lion Breweries Ltd
202. Bryan Storey Motors Ltd
203. Mr G. Aldrich,
     Far East Yacht
     Specialists Ltd
204. Robert Wynn-Parke,
     Wordcom Services Ltd
205. Neuchatel Swiss General
     Insurance Co. Ltd
206. Mr R.W. Inglis,
     John H. Walker & Co. Ltd
207. Vic Slade,
     AHI Flexible and Paper
     Products Group
208. Mr M.J. Faiers,
     Lion Breweries Ltd
209. Todd Phillips,
     Lightolier Manufact. Ltd
210. Mr W.S.W. Carruthers,
     Broadlands Financial
     Services
211. Mr J.H.G. Hare
212. Institute of Sport
213. Banks Peninsula Cruising
     Club
214. J.B. Carline,
     Paving Plant & Processes
215. Sandspit Yacht Club
216. Countrywide Building
     Society
217. Rotary Club of Taihape
218. S.G. & R.J. Morgan,
     Morgan Hire and
     Electrical Services
219. DMM Advertising
220. W. Sutherland,
     Sutherland Transport Ltd
221. R.H. Champion,
     Elroy Construction Ltd
222. David T. Scott
223. Probert Industries Ltd
224. Richard Melville,
     Melville Developments
225. Charter Cruise Co. Ltd
226. McKee Real Estate
227. Brian Franklin Cars Ltd
228. Mr & Mrs Trevor Sandes
229. Bowring Burgess Marsh
     & McLennan
230. Boyd Line Ltd
231. Rexim Trading Co. Ltd
232. Visual Compositions Ltd
233. Variant Owners Assn
234. Morris N. Amos,
     C.N.G. Mixer Co. Ltd
235. Mr & Mrs J.N. Taylor
236. Royal New Zealand
     Yacht Squadron
237. Robert A.W. des Tombe,
     Des Tombe Gifford & Co.

238. A.J. & J.G. Dickie
239. Kentucky Auto Dealers Ltd
240. Mr M. Rae
241. Feltex Ropes
242. Royal Port Nicholson
     Yacht Club
243. M.G. Ormsby
244. D.G. Ormsby
245. Mr M.P. Stubbing,
     IPSCO Ltd
246. Roger Manthel,
     Manthel Motors Ltd
247. J.W. Clague
248. Tim Bailey,
     Continental Car Services
249. Ian Margan,
     Margate Developments
250. Mr L.W. Tattersfield
251. Messrs. R. Muir &
     K. Turbott
252. Mr J. Hughes,
     General Finance Ltd
253. P.B. Coote
254. Mr H.L. White
255. Mr B.S. Robertson,
     Robertsons Ltd
256. Mr N.M. Newcomb,
     Neville Newcomb Ltd
257. Mr John Tennant
258. E.C. & J.F.L. Cave
259. Admiral Sir Gordon Tait
260. Douglas B. Foote,
     Douglas B. Foote Ltd
261. Mr S.J. Graham
262. Frank Casey,
     Frank Casey Ltd
263. Frank Perry,
     Perry Motors Ltd
264. Murray Smith,
     General Finance Ltd
265. Mr R.B. Cameron,
     R. Cameron & Co. Ltd
266. Mr D.N. Maxwell
267. Mr D.W. Cooper,
     Cooper Henderson
     Motors Ltd
268. Mr M.G. Neale,
     M.G. Neale & Co.
269. Bob Davie,
     Wang Computer Ltd
270. Mr & Mrs P. Turner
271. Mr & Mrs K.G. Batkin
272. Mr R.A. Sebelin,
     Fabco Industries Ltd
273. Mr M.L. Jones,
     Showerite Shower
     Screens (NZ) Ltd
274. John H. Heaslip,
     Union Carbide NZ Ltd
275. Mr K.V. Hills,
     AHI Metal Containers
     Group

276. Mr G.H.J. Hogg,
     Databank Systems Ltd
277. Mr G.R.J. Tedcastle,
     UEB Industries Ltd
278. Sir Robertson Stewart,
     PDL Industries Ltd
279. Alex Tulloch,
     Indosuez NZ Ltd
280. Willis Faber, PCL
281. A.W. Bryant Ltd
282. David Barker
283. Mr M.R. Upton
284. Mr P.S. Yates,
     Yates Corporation Ltd
285. Bucklands Beach Yacht
     Club
286. Ross Thomas Ellery
287. Bank of New Zealand
288. Mr & Mrs H. Day
289. Smith & Nephey (NZ) Ltd
290. Horace R. Kornegay,
     Rothmans Industries Ltd
291. M.E. & H.F.J. Van der Zwet
292. Peter & Laurie Buckley
293. Mr L.A. Turville
294. Mr R.G. Sutherland,
     Whitcoulls Ltd
295. Bill & Mark Hansen
296. Cancelled
297. Ross P. Millar
298. Marlin Metal &
     Machinery Ltd
299. J.P.R. Manoy
300. Garry de Joux Ltd
301. Bill Gibbons
302. David & Sandra Pinker,
     Marine Services (NSN) Ltd
303. J. Carey,
     Carey's Boatyard Ltd
304. Chris Hensley,
     Hensley & Moore Ltd
305. Bruce Lund,
     C. Lund & Son Ltd
306. Winston Day
307. Nelson Yacht Club
308. Mr J.R. Ramsay,
     John R. Ramsay Ltd
309. Robert A. Owens
310. Mr M.M. Langley
311. Judith Gimblett
312. Lt. Col R.M. Bell, MBE, ED
313. A.C. Hatrick (NZ) Ltd
314. Onerahi Yacht Club
315. Rob Duckworth,
     Lloyd Duckworth Ltd
316. John Fairhall,
     Archibald Motors Ltd
317. Panmure Yacht & Boating
     Club
318. Nelson & Gay Drummond

319. Mr L.P. Evans,
     Repco Corp NZ Ltd
320. NZ Forest Products Ltd
321. A.E. & V.H. Youell
322. Mr L. Grey,
     Nu-Look Windows
     (NZ) Ltd
323. Allen Howell,
     Odyssey Enterprises
324. Mr & Mrs R. van Borssum
325. Kevyn D. Moore,
     Weldwell (NZ) Ltd
326. Napier Sailing Club
327. Vogtherr family,
     Hastings Bacon Co. Ltd
328. Dominion Adjusters
     (Wellington) Ltd
329. Maupuia Hospital
330. Bob's Marine Ltd
331. Mayfair Caterers
332. Neville Stewart
333. Bryan family

334. Michael Francis Ltd
335. Rex Gillman,
     Pedlars' Recyclers
336. John & Jeanette Saunders
337. Hector Parton
338. Barrie Blackley,
     Gordon Harcourt &
     Blackley Ltd
339. Charles Ashton Ltd
340. Wairakei Motordrome
341. Mr N.F. Bramwell
342. Frederick Chandler
343. Wales & Co. (NZ) Ltd
344. Wilson Neill Ltd
345. Alastair Bisley
346. The Coffee Pot
347. Independent Taverns
348. Comalco NZ Ltd
349. Ted Nobbs,
     Stephenson & Turner
     (Sydney) Pty Ltd
350. John Keeley

351. Mr H.L. Julian, JP
352. Clive Bennett,
     Mogal Corporation Ltd
353. Rodger Fisher,
     Mogal Corporation Ltd
354. Bob Silvester,
     Owens Group Ltd
355. YKK Zippers
356. The Dominion Paint
     Centre Ltd
357. Air New Zealand Ltd
358. Air New Zealand Ltd
359. Mr & Mrs P. Cottle
360. Peter Rachtman,
     South Pacific Associates
361. Canterbury Internat. Ltd
362. Havelock North Club
363. J.N. Sunderland,
     Jason Products Ltd
364. Roy R. Ladd,
     Meredith Connell & Co.
365. Milk Promotion Board

Admiral's Club Members

Norm Barry & Robert Gordon, Barrycourt
  Motor Inn
Lindsay Beaver, Cooper Henderson Motors
Peter Brown, Avis Rent-a-Car
Mr Brown & Mr Hagaman, Innkeepers
John Butterfield, John W. Butterfield Ltd
Michael Clark, Michael Clark Ltd
Chris Curley, Ceramco Limited
Shane Evans, Forum Construction
Paul Fisher, J.R. Butland Prop. Ltd
Mr J.W. Foreman, Trigon Industries
Mr K.S. French, Versatile Garages Ltd
Goldfield Special School
David Gould, Gould Photographics
Alex Holmes, Farmers Trading Co.
Radio Lakeland
David Levene, Levene & Co. Ltd
Alan McArtney, Motorcorp
Les McGrath, NZI Video Network
Radio Nelson
Mr J.M. Paynter, Paynter Holdings Ltd
Brian Robbins, Robbins Holdings Ltd
Brian Simons, Simons Furnishing
Ray Thurston, Ray Thurston Ltd
Trevor Tobin, Sunline Homes Ltd
Dr L.L. Treadgold
Gavin Treadgold
Tim & Prue Wallis, Alpine Helicopters Ltd
Mr A.C. Worrallo, Selflok-Worrallo

Former *Ceramco* shareholders who transferred their interest to *Lion*

Kenneth D. Butland
Jim Wood & David Lee
Elysium & Unicorn Syndicate
Citizens of Nelson
Arthur O. Baldock
Robert A. Owens
Mr G. Forsyth & Mr W. Wood
Quality Bakers (HB) Ltd
Auckland Plastics Syndicate
Mr A.N. Harvey
Brookbanks Bros
City of Napier
Baron Ralph von Kohorn
J.B. Hay
Les & Graham Castles
The Electric Construction Co.
  of NZ Ltd
Manukau Timber Co. Ltd
J.E. Langley & P.C. Feltham
Table 1 Syndicate
  (Whispers II)
Peter Coote
R.J. Cox & T.R. Coxon
Mr W.M. Kember,
  Produce Markets Ltd
New Zealand Optical Ltd
Nu-Look Windows E/C Ltd
K.J. & A.C. Laird
E.A. Moody & P.G. Spackman
D.R. & B.J. Winstanley
Gavin Wright
L.R. Allen
John & Catherine Edwards
Barbara M. Nolan
Phase 2 Owners Syndicate
A.F. Fish
Messrs. Peterson, Rosenberg,
  Page, Plummer, Blair
G.W. Blithe
Doreen A. Anderson
The Manawatu Standard Ltd
Robertsons Ltd
Mr Q. Simpson
Airport Inn
Endeavour Services Corp. Ltd
New Lynn RSA Syndicate
Mr & Mrs L.D. Fenton
A.J. & M.M. Sheard
Timaru Yacht & Powerboat
  Club (No. 1 Syndicate)
C.M. Aitkenhead & Sons Ltd
The City of Wellington
Mainzeal Corporation Ltd
Nylex Fletcher Ltd
Mr G.C. Inwood
Mr & Mrs Les Hutchins
Bowater Motors (1980) Ltd
Mr Graham Stimpson
UEB Industries Ltd

Heards Ltd
Nathans Jet Set Travel Ltd
Mr C.E. Fordham
Moyes & Groves Ltd
Premier Plastics Ltd
Ajax Fasteners
Mr & Mrs A.F. Laity
Deloitte Haskins & Sells
Banks Peninsula Cruising Club
  Syndicate
Mr G.T. Durrant
Robert Fenwick
Mr Z. Milich,
  Sonny Elegant Knitwear Ltd
John H. Dale
The Unclutchables
R.L., S.E. & G.R. Allport
Wanganui Sailing Club
Mr & Mrs C.K. & P.P. Woodhead
L.E.G. Richardson
J.L., J.K., H.J.O. & H.A. Lusk
Tokoroa Yacht Club Syndicate
Tamaki Yacht Club Syndicate
Mr & Mrs J. Glanville
James Hardie & Co. Pty Ltd
John & Els Vandersyp
Mr & Mrs A.T. Gibbs
Warren Tuohey,
  Welcome Homes Ltd
Diana M. Walker,
  Autocrat Sanyo Ltd
The First Dockyard Syndicate
Ralph Roberts
Mr A.F. Hall
Mr T. Maxwell de Denne
Mr B.W. Ewing
Mr J.H. Taylor & P.A. Rigg
Jack McIntyre
Colin & Neil Wakefield
Jordan, Sandman Smythe & Co.
Mr W.A. Laurie
Kenneth & Joy Webley
Randall J. Peat
Mr R.H. Walker,
  Autocrat Sanyo Ltd
Charlie & Trish Webley
Banks Peninsula Cruising Club
Takapuna Boating Club
Mr D.R. Levene
NZ Express Transport Ltd
Mr C.R. Bidwill,
  Ceramco Ltd
Sea Nymph Boats Ltd
Messrs B. Bean & J. Field
Devonport Yacht Club
Devonport Yacht Club,
  — Executive Syndicate No. 1
Devonport Yacht Club,
  — Executive Syndicate No. 2

H. & J. Towle
Sarah Easen & The Lake
  Taupo Yacht Club
William Ritchie
Mr D.J. Alison
Mr J.W. McKenzie
Mr G.F. Gair
Mr G.W. Dunsford
Mr J.M. Foster
Mr D.H. Scott
Mr H.L. Julian
Mr L.W. Tattersfield
Mr J.A. Carmichael
Peter J. Faire
Mr L.H. Julian
Lake Taupo Yacht Club
Mr P.J. Cornes
Mr R.B. Waddell
Mr M.H. Wiseman
Miss M.M. McNeil
Mr D.P. Winstone
Harry & Nora Foster
A.B. Griffin
Royal N.Z. Yacht Squadron
Mr R.W. Massey
Diversey Wallace Ltd
Team McMillan Ford
Kenneth W. Staton
The Waitemata Syndicate
Mr D.L. Hazard
The Crew of Ceramco Ltd
Flag Ship Committee of Royal
  N.Z. Yacht Squadron
Mr J. Gifford
Goodyear NZ Ltd
Nirvana Syndicate
Outboard Boating Club of
  Auckland Inc
Richmond/Webb Syndicate
Amco Oil Syndicate
Auckland Co-op Taxi Society Ltd
Ross Roofing Ltd
South Auckland Caravan Centre
Olga M. Faire & Peter R. Moule
Gerald S. Hall
Sheila Glendining
Mr C.W. Reynolds
Eight O'Clock Newspapers,
  NZ News Ltd
NZ Cement Holdings
Rhumb Raider Syndicate
Mr D.W. Hurley
Sir Robertson Stewart, CBE,
  PDL Holdings Ltd
Mr H.T.W. Nolan
Fruit Distributors Ltd
Messrs Haughton, McRae,
  McRae, Powell, Larsen

Kapiti Boating Club Inc.
  No. 3 Syndicate
Peter Shorter,
  Shorters Car Distributors Ltd
Mr & Mrs B. & J. Blake
Mr P.J. Blake
Auckland Motor Yacht Club
Barker Textiles Ltd
Dr & Mrs G. & V. Beacham
Broadbank Corporation Ltd
Cox & Dawes Ltd
Foveaux Crossing Syndicate
Bill Gibbons
E.C. Dewhirst & D.C. Holdaway
Gerhard Ammermann,
  Bayer NZ Ltd
Joyce S. Dowsett
Messrs McCulloch & Menzies,
  Wellington Moths Syndicate
Rheem NZ Ltd
Kapiti Boating Club No. 2 Synd.
Mr W.L. Murphy
Leonard & Dingley Ltd
Buttle Wilson & Co. Ltd
Christopher T. Horton
Healing Industries Ltd

Papatoetoe Rotary Club
  Members Syndicate
Eileen J. Greenhalgh
Embecon Pty Ltd
Charles Wiffen Ltd
Warren Blake
Mr W.G. Beckett
Avondale RSA Syndicate
Bill Savidan,
  Craddock Fibreglass Ltd
Mr H.J. Bull
Peter R. Brown
Mr & Mrs G.C. Leitch & family
The Children of Goldfields
  Special School
Trevor Burton
H.E. Buchanan
Durafort Investments Ltd
Messrs. Stevens, Cowie, Chilton,
  Stewart, Potts & Sons
EDP Operations Syndicate
Richard Jamieson
John Gault Syndicate
Mr T.H. Leys
H.W. Smith Ltd

SWAPD Syndicate,
  Shell Oil NZ Ltd
A.H. Irwin & M.J. Walsh
Independent Newspapers Ltd
Lotus 9.2 Association
Kapiti Boating Club No. 1 Synd.
Read & Gibson Ltd
Comalco Extrusions Ltd
Nona E. Ross
C.J. Lovegrove
Mr J.R. Williams,
  Production Engineering Co. Ltd
Mrs J. Trotter
Marsden Alexander Motors Ltd
Willis Toomey Robinson & Co.
Carter Holt Holdings Ltd
Porirua City Council
Chinaman Syndicate
Russell G. Ellis
Waitaki NZ Refrigerating Ltd
Clive Manners-Wood &
  Don Abel
Mr W.N. White
Royal NZ Navy Sailing Club Inc
  C/- H.M.N.Z.S. Tamaki
Williams & Kettle Ltd